Personal, Social and Moral Education

to the memory of Ann Sedgwick (1916-1993)

Say, wast thou conscious of the tears I shed?

- William Cowper, 'On the Receipt of my Mother's Picture Out of Norfolk'

PERSONAL, SOCIAL AND MORAL EDUCATION

Fred Sedgwick

David Fulton Publishers
London

David Fulton Publishers Ltd
2 Barbon Close, London WC1N 3JX

First published in Great Britain by
David Fulton Publishers 1994

Note: The right of Fred Sedgwick to be identified as the author of this work has been asserted by him in accordance with the Copyright, Designs and Patents Act 1988.

British Library Cataloguing in Publication Date

A catalogue record for this book is available from the British Library

ISBN 1-85346-291-8

Typeset by Harrington & Co., London
Printed in Great Britain by BPC Books and Journals Ltd., Exeter

Contents

Acknowledgements

My acknowledgements are due to the following, who gave advice, or provided raw material for case studies: Dawn Sedgwick, Mary Jane Drummond, Paula Sorhaindo, Jo Palmer, Dennis Ruston, Henry Burns Eliot, Alan Parkinson, Annabelle Dixon, Stephanie Lacey, Maureen Hutchins, Melissa Stockdale, Zoe Mair, Martin Castle, Daniel Sedgwick, Jacquie and Simon Knott, John Langdon, Alan Shoote, John Lynch, Joan Webster, Sue Mulvaney, Seamus Fox, Marilyn Hamilton, Peter Moore, John Cotton, Marie McKenna and Maureen Costello.

I apologise to anyone I have inadvertently missed.

Teachers at the following schools gave me hospitality as a researcher:

Cavell First, Norwich; Holdbrook CP, Waltham Cross, Hertfordshire.

Teachers at other schools also helped me in many ways, especially Kexborough Primary School, Barnsley. Others were:

Combs First School, Stowmarket; The Old Rectory Montessori Nursery School, Woodbridge, Suffolk; Saxmundham Middle, Suffolk; All Saints VACP School, Lawshall, Bury St Edmunds, Suffolk; Downing Primary, Ipswich; Sprites Junior, Ipswich; Murrayfield Primary, Ipswich; St Mary's, Ipswich; Feltwell Elementary School, RAF Feltwell.

Earlier versions of six of the paragraphs in this book have appeared in *Montessori Education* and *The Times Educational Supplement*. The unattributed quotations at the beginnings of the introduction and chapter seven come from my poem 'National Curriculum' (*Lies*, Headland 1991).

Preface

The title I wanted for this book was *Just Education*.

A pun, of course. As I was collecting case studies and writing, it became clear that, first, my work was about the whole of education, rather than any bolted-on newcomer; and that, second, it was about justice or, as most children say, fairness. The act of putting these two ideas together made it clear that my book was about something even more than the sum of these. It was about being a learning human being in a social world we constantly define and re-define as fair or unfair, as just and unjust.

So *Just Education*.

But my publishers said that as a title, that was a good idea that wouldn't work. Nice one, as they say – but no. They'd got a point, as publishers always have: I've tripped up before on snappy titles that don't say enough about what's between the covers. So it's *Personal, Social and Moral Education*.

But I want to say at the outset that justice is central to any consideration of this topic, and in the end the book has simply become a book about education: *just* education.

Ipswich
August 1994

The Primary Curriculum Series

This innovative series promotes reflective teaching and active forms of pupil learning. The books explore the implications of these commitments for curriculum and curriculum-related issues.

The argument of each book flows in, around and among a variety of case studies of classroom practice, introducing them, probing, analysing and teasing out their implications before moving on to ther next stage of the argument. The case study material varies in source and form – children's work, diary entries, drawings, poetry, literature, interviews. The vitality and richness of primary school practice are conveyed, together with the teacher expertise on which these qualities are based.

Series Editors

Mary Jane Drummond is Tutor in Education, University of Cambridge Institute of Education, and Andrew Pollard is Professor in the Faculty of Education, University of the West of England, Bristol.

Series Titles

Introduction: A way in

...they sit in classrooms as the day
like a bright green-skirted angel
drifts through light and stirred shadows...

On the wall of the entrance hall of the first school, there are about twenty A4-size children's paintings based on works by Seurat and Monet. 'We have been looking', says a notice, 'at paintings by famous artists...' There's also a card displayed so you can't miss it. It's headed RULES IN OUR SCHOOL and ends AGREED BY PUPILS SEPTEMBER 1993.

'Entrance hall' is a bit grand, in fact. There's evidence that constraints of size mean that this area is used as classroom overflow. But the signatures on the bottom of RULES are genuine children's writing. Some of the rules and sanctions have a disturbingly authentic ring, too. The headteacher says to me later, 'We update them every year... We have to restrain some of the more excessive punishments the children on the School's Council suggest... '

In the second school there is a similar notice, but it has been done as a sampler by a parent, and it's neatly framed. The rules are much the same, being about respect for property, the unacceptability of bullying, and the right to teach and to learn, in that order. The headteacher says later, 'Oh yes, we take PSE seriously here'. This entrance hall is part of a corridor, but it has a free, uncramped feel about it. A child says to me, 'Are you the poet?' All sorts of smart answers cross my mind, like, I was last month when I wrote a poem, or, I hope so. 'Yes', I say. 'Can you tell me where the headteacher's room is?'

In the third school, there is a shining display about a local but dead poet, William Cowper. It includes photocopies – of his handwriting, of contemporary drawings of the house where he spent the last years of his life, of portraits. Someone has typed, on an old-fashioned machine, twenty-four lines from one of the poet's most famous poems. A child holding dinner registers looks up at these lines as I watch. Someone else (the name is supplied on a neatly inscribed card) has handwritten an account of the poet's life, neglecting his three attacks of melancholia, the results, it has been argued, of a combination of manic depression and Calvinistic theology. On one of these occasions he tried, with almost comic unsuccess, to hang himself. During another, he wrote the first lines of his lyric poem, 'Light shining out of darkness': 'God moves in a mysterious way/His wonders to perform'.

In this same entrance hall there are settees, beige-coloured non-slip floors partially hidden by a dark brown rug, and drapes covering the lefthand lower corner of the display. There is also a group of pot plants. The effect is handsome and middle-class. I open a door off the entrance hall and step into a more familiar setting. It may be the library, it may be the dining hall. Whatever it is, it has an air of simultaneous multi- and dis-use. There are shelves of books with coloured stickers at the base of their spines, and there are tables covered with formica. There are other tables folded neatly against the wall. It is what the deputy head will later describe to me as 'the dining hall-stroke-library'.

In another school, the fourth, I wait in what must have been the space where hunters tugged off their boots in the early nineteenth century. All around, among the sea prints and reproductions of paintings of boats drawn up on the beach at Sheringham, are signed photographs of a famous princess. I wait (I have an appointment) fantasising briefly about being Frederick Wentworth expecting Anne Elliot to come downstairs any minute, after all the misunderstandings have been explained. I imagine the clatter of a Saturday around what I would call teatime in Jane Austen's time. In 1993, girls in uniform clothes move across the hall in clashing directions. Later I ask a teacher why a famous princess is framed everywhere. 'She is an old girl of the school ... she is remembered most because she won the best kept pet competition every year she was here...'

What emerges from these experiences is a theme that will persist throughout this book: concealment. We hide from children certain excesses – lunacy in an eighteenth century poet, for example. We disguise from parents and journalists – and anyone else who might have some effect on our school's financial well-being – what lies behind the shining displays in the entrance hall. Step through what appears to be the gate to the best of good lives, and you find 'dining rooms-stroke-libraries', 'gents' lavatories-stroke-store houses'. In one way, this isn't a problem. What house doesn't have its glory hole? But in schools we pretend that all is surface. We are like the teacher (and we are all potentially this teacher, I suspect) who buries the dead rabbit discreetly on Friday evening when the children have gone home, and buys another identical one on Saturday morning, to conceal the first one's death. Hiding the messiness of learning has become more and more important in the last fifteen years, as schools have been required to be presentable first and educational second. The headteacher who cracks the boiler code, and manages to heat only the entrance hall, while leaving the rest of the school in a frugal chill, will soon be miles ahead in the PR race, as well as financially better off.

Of course, hiding realities is just one aspect of a wider phenomenon observable in the adult world at large. Frank Tuohy (1976) tells us, in his account of the first production of J. M. Synge's play *The Playboy of the Western World* at the Abbey Theatre in Dublin, which concerns life, death and love in the low rural areas of the west of Ireland:

> The pious who barracked and jeered...were only two or three blocks away from 'Monto', the worst slum in Europe, the brothel area that James Joyce called 'Nighttown'...Yeats remembered 'Synge came and stood beside me, and said, "A young doctor has just told me that he can hardly keep himself from jumping on to a seat, and pointing out in that howling mob those whom he is treating for venereal disease"'

An ability to pretend that everything in the universe is clean and decent when a brothel flourishes yards away has its equivalents in all aspects of life, including education.

A central thread in PSME is how we can teach each other to face realities, and how we accept that facing up to anything is never easy, never something that can be trained. It is never a skill. But in teaching facing up is central, because to *teach* is, etymologically, to *show*. Thus, if we want children to live lives that are moral, concealment can have no part in our teaching.

4

In 1987, three years before I left my third and final headship, an adviser responsible for Home Economics wondered if I would join a group of other advisers, teachers and headteachers writing guidelines for Personal and Social Education. It may seen shameful now for me to admit that I'd never heard of PSE. This was to be one of those odd, breakneck periods of learning, where one moves from ignorance, through recognition, to an evangelical commitment, inside a matter of months. This move also involved, at first, an understanding of what I came to see as the establishment view of PSE (at least as seen by my local authority's committee); then a dissatisfaction with that view; and, finally, the slow crystalising of another option. It also meant a realisation that there is some truth in what nearly all primary headteachers say when asked what do they do about PSE: 'We do it all the time, we don't need curriculum slots for it, all our work is about PSE, it's about the way we treat children, isn't it?'

But first I had to face a phenomenon known to all teachers. Curriculum today is like a creaking shelf. Every year, two or three more volumes are plonked on it, and you wonder what's going to drop off the other end, but nothing does. You think you've got on top of most of your responsibilities, though you are aware of a few things at the corner of your mind that you haven't even started thinking about yet. Thus, over the past fifteen years, we have learned the importance of working with parents, working with bilingual pupils, the introduction of micro-technology, the development of multicultural and anti-racist principles, the growth of health and sex education, and developments in oracy and literacy. Twenty-five years ago, in contrast, I got by in my first job with reading, writing, arithmetic (though we called it maths), nature study, painting and PE; and a few Bible stories. The whole thing stopped on Thursday mornings after play for *En Avant* ('Je m'appelle M. Sedgwick...Comment t'appelle-tu?...' 'Je m'appelle Michelle...').

However shameful my ignorance and prejudice about PSE were at the time ('Oh no, we've got something else to do now'), it still seems to me to be forgivable. The curriculum locomotive (to change my metaphor) I was supposed to be driving in 1987 often stuttered under the weight of all those carriages; now I was supposed to take on PSE and (worse) I had to go back to school and couple up my colleagues' engines to it as well. And, with hindsight, it certainly seems wrong that, in this local authority, PSE was subsumed inside Home Economics, a traditionally low-grade subject in terms of advisory responsibility, a subject that still raised sniggers among the new, macho, management brigade of headteachers. I demurred at the adviser's invitation, as I always did. I knew I'd be asked to join committees where, having searched every crevice of County Hall tarmac looking for a parking space, I would be required to wear a tie, and sit still for hours, sulkily inspecting 'documents'.

But a week or two later I joined the group. It comprised an officer, three headteachers (one secondary, one middle, and me, representing primary schools); two or three advisers; and an ex-primary head. There was also an officer concerned with accountability above all else, an expert with minutes, a devil in the committee skirmish. Within two years the group had finished its work, and had produced its *Guidelines*. This excellent booklet divided PSE into three main parts:

- the styles of teaching and quality of learning

- the explicitly planned curriculum

- relationships, attitudes and values

(Suffolk CC undated)

These three components taken together made up what the booklet called the school's 'ethos'. The rest of the material comprised notes on developing a 'systematic approach' which involved a curriculum audit. This latter activity involved five stages:

- preparing the audit

- preparing the staff

- carrying out the audit

- data analysis

- detailed investigation.

The idea was to produce a table of necessary components for PSE. These included:

- Work-related activities in the classroom

- Work experience/placement

- Planned activities outside school

- The community as a learning resource

and these were ticked off in small boxes under columns headed with all the subjects of the curriculum. The discussion in the group had enthused me about PSE. My colleagues were passionate evangelicals for their subject, and I came to respect their knowledge and experience. We received material about schools that had re-designed whole curricula in terms of PSE. One infant school 'delivered' (their document's term for it) everything 'in terms of six topics – Ourselves, Home, School, Outdoors, Events and People'.

But the idea of 'auditing' reduced me to despair. How could love, death and the whole damn thing – life, let alone the good life – be reduced to a pools coupon? Also, the preparatory steps outlined above seemed to be just that: preparatory. One got ready for the audit, and did it: but the audit was only preparatory to finding out what you weren't dealing with: a huge, delaying deficit model. When would one *teach* PSE? Preparing for the audit and the audit itself both got in the way of curriculum, much as managerial concerns frequently seemed to be deflecting attention from educational ones. The question of learning, its presence or its absence, was being hidden. As John White (in his 1990 book *Education and the Good Life*) says, 'The nature of morality...is deeply problematical'. These problems were masked by the simplistic lists, much as they are denied by ideologues who insist that we all know the difference between right and wrong, and all that matters is enforcing right and punishing wrong.

Indeed, it later emerged that so much work that passed for PSE effectively kept consideration of the subject out of the classroom, where the children might engage, closely, actively, with conviction, with what often are, after all, very controversial issues: love, work, pleasure, pain, death. This was how I came to see emphasis on displays in corridors, welcoming headteachers' offices, with soft toys dropped carefully, casually, 'pleasingly' around chairs and floors. This was how I came to see so-called child-centred schools that, behind the disguise, were run as little one-party states, the headteacher, of course, being the unelected supremo. This was also how I came to see those entrance halls. Even though it is received wisdom that a school teaching PSE well has to have a welcoming way in, I became used to asking: what is all this show and surface hiding? What's behind the closed doors? What's the cover-up covering up?

Suddenly the words 'PSE policy' emerged as, at worst, destructive and, at best, procrastinatory. I'd sensed this whenever any school I worked in was about to be inspected or (same thing, softer rhetoric) reviewed. For some weeks before the advisers or inspectors turned up, teaching took a lower priority than writing 'documents'. Now I could see policies, audits and all the rest of a time-consuming managerial apparatus blocking the teaching, blocking the learning, placing the classroom and what happens there lower down the scale of significance than hessian-clad corridors and comfortable G Plan libraries.

Also, the word 'delivery' as used in the six-topic infant school's PSE plans made me nervous. My conviction, growing from work on an MA course on applied research in education, that educational moments are at their most potent when both partners – teachers and students – are learning, had led me to dismiss talk of delivery as a false, commercialised model of education that distorts its empowering, potentially subversive nature. The fashionable notion that learning was no more problematical than a visit to the supermarket – with the core subjects, English, Mathematics and Science, as meat; the foundation subjects as vegetables; and everything else as trimmings – made me feel embattled but confident in what I held as a nobler model. I wasn't going to be happy accepting PSE (of all educational areas the most concerned with the messiness of being human) as something that teachers *deliver*.

The Suffolk authority generously sent me on a residential course on PSE run by the Department of Education and Science (as it was then). There were two themes in this course. The first was an emphasis on Health Education. It was clear that much work had been done by writers working for the Health Education Authority. Indeed, as an adviser responsible for PSE said to me, many schools worked on the assumption that PSE and Health Education were the same thing. This assumption depends to a large extent on what has been called 'the curriculum of moral panics'. We see young women beginning smoking, we see the destruction of personalities and social units through the agency of drugs, we anticipate what effects AIDS might have on the next generation. So, understandably, we design programmes, activities, worksheets, tutorial sessions, to make a stand against these unhealthy factors.

The problem with this approach is that, for example, in trying to prevent young women smoking, we are often seen by those young women as denying their autonomy. The PSE educator has to find ways of improving the quality of life while somehow ensuring that pupils retain, indeed increase, their purchase on their own lives and their critical decisions, especially when these are issues of health. The emphasis on respect for property in many sets of school rules pinned up in entrance halls is a symptom of another aspect of panicking PSE. Even worse, this emphasis places assaults on human beings at a lower level than assaults on their bags and the school walls.

The second strand of the DES course was the advocacy of what I later came to define as the 'hessian and teazle single party state'. One headteacher-type I collide with these days is the teazle autocrat, or triple-mounter. This head is obsessed with display. When he was a classroom teacher, he spent hours standing in front of carpeting-covered boxes, moving glazed pots tiny distances and shifting triple-mounted pictures on the hessian-backed wall a millimetre or two till the effect was what he termed 'aesthetically pleasing'. Now that he is in charge, the competitive element introduced by recent legislation, which turns presentation into substance, is a further force behind his obsession.

Part of the hessian/presentability/teazle strand on the DES course was a workshop on calligraphy subtitled 'Handwriting and Display Matters'. This, in the opinion of several participants, sold the life, love and death issues that PSE is concerned with desperately short. A popular word was 'ethos', and when one headteacher asked HMI running the course whether this ethos should be the child-centred one that had been HMIs' ideology since 1967, or the government's current one of competition, he was told 'I'm going to put that question on hold', and the issue was, as an adviser put it in her report to her authority afterwards, 'diligently avoided'. If the good life is a matter of personal autonomy in a participative democracy; if the central problem of a national curriculum is how we might increase *our* autonomy without destroying that of our fellow citizens; then emphasis on health only, and on ethos as soft toy or pleasing display will get us nowhere.

One of the most depressing effects of these ways of looking at PSME is that controversial issues will be sunk in a sea of middle class values and spurious objectives. For example, it was difficult in this setting to give multicultural or anti-racist issues their full weight. When I mentioned anti-racism during the committee's deliberations, I was asked not to 'hi-jack the group on to a single issue'. But this single issue was crucial then, and recent attacks on racial minorities in this country, racist murders in playgrounds, and the election of a British National Party candidate in local elections in Millwall, London, have made it arguably one of the most important issues facing teachers today.

There has been a shift in my thinking since 1990 that makes the extra adjective 'moral' central to any consideration of PSE. The book offers an analysis of the key questions that make up PSME: What is a person? a good person? What – to use a term from philosophy – is the good life? What do we mean by integrity? In that word, two concepts meet. First, coherence. Do things – different classrooms, different subject areas, different attitudes – cohere in a school? Is life in some way integrated? And secondly, honesty. Is the school as close to being honest as it can be, or is it a school in hiding – hiding its real work behind a wall of PR and double mounting? Some headteachers, obsessed with the first of these two concepts, make their schools cohere by concealing educational messiness, and demanding the neat pre-packed NC-friendly evidence required by inspectors, central government and the media.

What do we mean by 'society'? What sort of society do we want to live in? Baroness Thatcher memorably said, when she was Mrs Thatcher and Prime Minister, that there was no such thing as society. Certainly there is much empty talk about 'community' ('the gay community', 'the Asian community') which appears to make solid what is fluid. But PSME is full of the implications of society, and mooting the possibility that we are merely a collection of individuals motivated by market forces is to depersonalise, to be anti-social, to be amoral, and to be uneducational.

This book is based on teachers and children talking, and on the analysis of children's work in all areas of the curriculum because, as John White (1990) persuasively argues:

> there should be no rift between the 'academic' side of a school and the 'personal/social' side, since academic aims should be underpinned by a concern for the pupils' well-being.

PSME is defined here (cumbersomely perhaps, but I need some sort of starting point) as:

the process by which teachers act to promote personal, moral and social ways of being and behaving; also qualities, attitudes and understanding.

It is the whole curriculum – after all, what is there except me and the rest of the world? Every scientific and technological project, every painting, every dance, every musical performance is a research project into the relationship between me and the rest of the world.

Thus, a child is 'doing PSME' when she

- looks into her own experience, feelings, sorrow or joy for the purpose of writing a poem
- draws an old person from life
- collaborates in a scientific experiment
- cooks a dinner
- helps another child who has fallen over
- listens to her teacher reading
- organises a game in which she and friends have to work together to meet a common objective

And the teacher is teaching PSME when s/he

- praises a child or a group of children
- helps a child to face up to some difficulty
- encourages a timid child to do something that seems (to the child) brave
- takes pains to ensure that girls as well as boys play with the lego
- teaches a story from the Koran
- brings the best out of a child in Drama

Look, for a more detailed example, at this piece of writing (uncorrected, as are all examples in this book, unless otherwise stated):

My eye can turn right round and I can see my brain and in my brain there are lots of little people working but in the night when I turn my eyes round the people are sleeping on bunk beds

but sometimes when I have no one to play with at school I take my eyes out and bounce them up and down and when grils come passing by they skrimm and shot miss shes taken her eyeball out so I quickly stuff it back in

and when Im bored at home of watching cartoons I take my eye out and through it out the window and it gos round the world and I see that in other places of the world it is much more exciting because there are aliens trying to take over the world

and when I feel it it feels like a pice of very flat paper so I just get a pencil and write a poem and I called it Ten lies about my eyes

There are many PSME issues that this writing raises. First, the teacher has not corrected all the spelling and grammar. If he had, that would have taught Saesha, the writer, a significant lesson about the importance of her thinking as compared with secretarial issues. It would have taught her that technical issues are paramount, and implied that content, made up of imagination, verbal dexterity and wit, is only taught to train our grammar. Second, the child has written with authentic verve, responding to a stimulus that has engaged her, rather than responding numbly to a stimulus following some writing exercise in a dead textbook that has had as much relationship to her life as a lump of moon rock. Third, in the last paragraph (if it is a paragraph) she has introduced a reflection on the nature of what she is doing.

There is another relevant issue here. A central theme of this introduction has been the conflict between openness and concealment. Saesha has been asked to write down lies about her eye. How can we square this with our earlier comments about openness and lack of hiding? We can do this by arguing that in one sense all art is a lie. Neither Anne Elliot, in *Persuasion*, nor the Big Friendly Giant existed, but in lying about them, Jane Austen and Roald Dahl told profound truths about pride, prejudice, sense, sensibility, love, family life, wit, compassion, violence, greed. Here Saesha has been freed from literal truth and this has allowed her to explore her relationship with her language ('they skrimm and shot'). She has also meditated on what it is like when she is alone, when she has 'no one to play with' and when she is 'bored at home'. As Picasso said somewhere, art is a lie told to tell the truth.

A newly qualified teacher argued that PSME wasn't everywhere: 'Take the maths curriculum, some of the algebraic stuff in maths at upper junior level...it's very hard to see PSE there, except the self-discipline bit and the bit about...presenting your work...in pages of algebra there is no real relationship there, in terms of PSE'. But even in exercises involving pure mathematics, worksheets can have all white children in the illustrations, or illustrations that recognise the racial richness of our society. A stanza from a found poem, 'Common Sense' by Alan Brownjohn (*Collected Poems* (1983)) demonstrates how even arithmetic has always had social and moral implications:

> A milk dealer buys milk at 3d a quart. He
> Dilutes it with 3% water and sells
> 124 gallons of the mixture at
> 4d per quart. How much of his profit is made by
> Adulterating the milk?
>> From *Pitman's Common Sense Arithmetic*, 1917

One might ask whether children should be doing things in school that cannot tolerate the label 'personal, educational, moral'.

The word 'whole' is critical in the sense that any work has to be involved with the whole school. You can't have successful PSME programmes that apply to only one class, or one year. But the word 'whole' suggests, secondly, that PSE is concerned with the whole person. In its useful response to the old National Curriculum Council in March 1989, the National Association for Pastoral Care in Education (NAPCE) outlined the various selves in the young human learner that PSE must address:

- bodily self...addressing the use and misuse of the body, including through substance abuse
- sexual self...
- social self...understanding others' perspectives
- vocational self...not simply 'career choice', but a wider look at what sort of contributing adult to become
- moral self...
- self as a learner...
- self in the organisation...

The problem here is that, as Peter Robinson says in the foreword to Delwyn and Eva Tattum's book *Social Education and Personal Development* (1992), we

> subscribe to a...rhetoric of educating 'the whole person', but in fact emphasise adult control and are more likely to preach about responsibilities than require pupils to exercise them. 'Personal and Social Education' was introduced more as an additional subject than as a pervasive principle. It is prone to be devalued as light relief from learning lessons.

Thus, as one twelve-year-old said to me, 'PSE is when you have your class teacher instead of your subject teacher'. An English adviser approached a truth when she commented sardonically that PSE was only what 'we've been doing in good secondary English for years': presumably discussing moral issues through the medium of literature.

One of the taken-for-granted concepts that the view of PSME elaborated in this book criticises is the notion of skills. This notion, like the notion of training, devalues the experiences that children are offered in a school, because it makes all one an infinite set of experiences of different values and difficulty. When we use the term 'social skills', we tend to reduce the making of friends to the level of riding a bike. An extreme example of this is 'prayer skills'. (My editor comments here that 'skill' is inappropriate for bikes too, and goes on to say: 'I must tell you about a nursery record I know that has 8 levels of "scooter skills"'). We need a better term than skills that doesn't lose sight of active, lived life. As a concept, 'skills' also has the disadvantage of atomising the whole. In effect it disintegrates the basic NAPCE model as given above.

I chose this way into this introduction through school entrance halls partly because it is received wisdom that teachers in schools that are conscious of PSE will do their best to make their buildings welcome to visitors. Now here is one more school and its welcome, before I try to show that it is what lies behind the welcoming entrance hall that counts.

It's a quarter to nine in the morning at a two hundred strong rural school, and there is a lot going on. Parents, children, teachers, and a milkman wanting his money mill around and wait. As you step into the bustling entrance hall, one door is closed against the noise of the beginning of a day. As the secretary and another adult field questions about dinner money, school trips and the forthcoming school car boot sale, you notice that the headteacher's office door remains closed.

It has a digital door lock. Every day he tells two or perhaps three colleagues what number he has chosen for that day. This morning, the secretary has not been elected as one of those people. She knows that he does not answer knocks. Later, once all the children are in class, the area education officer turns up unannounced to see the headteacher. The deputy head, who knows the combination because she has an appointment with him at midday, is out on a morning's visit to a local shop with her class. The secretary doesn't know who else has the number, and the headteacher doesn't respond to knocking. She and the visitor crossly and intermittently monitor the area outside the room and eventually ambush the headteacher – clearly a man well aware of the power of silence and non-communication – when he finally needs the lavatory.

This is clearly a school suffering from an advanced and extreme form of the rampant managerial neurosis that sees what goes on in the headteacher's room – LMS printouts, PR leaflets, telephone conversations with colleagues in the National Association of Heateachers – as more important than what happens in classrooms. The practice of this school is teaching a powerful PSME lesson to whoever comes in through the front door. Sometimes the headteacher sends a note round to the staff: 'Emergencies only today, please'.

All this is, critically, PSE – or, as we must now call it, PSME. What, we might ask, is the headteacher hiding? So, too, is the following story. Two teachers are talking at a lunch party given by a third teacher for her son, who was taught by one of the first two teachers. Both of them – men – are responsible in their respective schools for English. Neither has any allowance. Both describe more senior teachers in their school engaged in all sorts of tasks: painting floors in rooms recently covered by new glass ceilings; organising fundays and dances; arranging car boot sales...

Mary Jane Drummond (in her 1993 book *Assessing Children's Learning*) writes about teachers and their perceptions of their responsibilities. She found that teachers frequently claim responsibility for an enormous number of large factors: 'the whole child ...the children...their parents...the headteacher...other staff... myself...' 'One reply,' Drummond records, 'includes "and future generations"'. Duties implicit in this data seem large enough. But now educational or even human responsibilities are given a lower status in some schools than presentational, organisational and managerial skills. Thus stories like the one about the combination lock are relevant to this book because of the messages about personal value and esteem that can be read in these real life experiences.

In chapter 4 on violence, I discuss how PSME issues are relevant to the way teachers deal with each other. Headteachers who send round notes at 9.00 a.m. saying 'Emergencies only today please' cannot hope to teach positive PSME to the children, though they will inadvertently teach many a negative PSME lesson. Authorities and governments who bully teachers will eventually find they must confront the generations of young adults they deserve. Throughout this book, there are implications for how adults in schools and in the increasingly distant and monolithic systems that govern schools, should behave. A personal, social, moral and educational rationale that only affects the powerless is a rationale for injustice.

Learners in a school where the teachers are fully engaged with all that PSME implies for learning processes will re-educate themselves and that school. They will learn again that the love of money is indeed the root of all evil. They will give power to themselves, both pupils and teachers, as they brush aside the trivial, the imitations of Impressionist painters, the warm welcomes to cold schools, the fundraising, the administrative – and educate again.

Learners in such a school will recognise that it has things to hide – who hasn't? – but it will suspect what those things are, and work towards exposing them to the critical light of collaborative educational thinking. It should go without saying that returning to educational values will help teachers to recover from the despair that afflicts even the youngest teachers. A newly qualified teacher told me at the end of her first year:

> My beliefs haven't changed at all, but my attitudes have, phenomenally. I think when I first started this year I thought I could put things right. I mean, I really believed I could put things right. And solve problems with them, using that sort of PSE-based approach. And now at the end of the year I would say it's much less of a part of my job than I thought, not because I want it to be but because that's just the way it pans out. And I've come to realise I can't do what I wanted to do at the beginning of the year.

You can do what you want to do. But you must put people and education first, and let the administrative catch up where it will.

In this book I offer two case studies. Then I describe how schools have dealt with the issues of birth and death. I suggest that we will find education (especially PSME) impossible unless we examine the ways children see and have seen their schools. I discuss issues of violence, gender and race, and try to open up the package to INSET. In conclusion, I reiterate themes that have persisted thoughout my book, and introduce another one, crucial and, finally, the only one that matters.

CHAPTER ONE

A human box

In the beginning was the word

St John 1.1

My box is made of people It is a humen box

Perry Lamprell (Holdbrook CP School)

This chapter takes the form of two case studies. I visited Holdbrook CP School, Hertfordshire and Cavell First School, Norwich and made extensive notes. Then I sent my notes to the headteachers, and later integrated their comments into my text. Another school, Kexborough Primary in Barnsley, regrettably, I never saw. I'd heard about it from my editor, and spoke at length to the headteacher on the phone. And then I received material from them that I incorporated into this chapter and also chapter 2. Again, I sent drafts to the headteacher.

I used a tape recorder at Holdbrook, and found the results technically less than useful. Perhaps a school as busy as Holdbrook is difficult to record in. On my second visit, I promoted my fallback method, notebook and shorthand, to first method. I always showed my notes to the teachers quoted. In the rest of this book I use case study material in a more fragmented way, finding innovative practice in areas related to, or grounded in, notions of PSME, and making notes as quickly as I could. Large parts of my data are the words of children, either written or spoken. Malcolm Ross said of a previous book of mine '...like Eliot's garden, the book is full of voices, mostly the voices of children...' ('Children's Vision', *Times Educational Supplement*, 19 March 1993). I am often surprised at how rarely that can be said of books about schools.

Kexborough PS has spelt out a curricular model. As I write, the current Secretary of State for Education has suggested that all schools should fly the Union Jack. Now, appropriately if fortuitously, this model resembles that flag in its construction: the subjects fill the triangles around the edge, and PSE is at the core.

Sue Mulvaney, headteacher at Kexborough, also sent me some clearly articulated school rules. The most striking moments in them are when we see children expressing their concerns with only the slightest adult interference. On the one hand, 'Do...Be pleased with yourself when you manage to complete a task or learn something new' and 'Do...As the teachers say' and 'Do...Stand still when the bell goes' are rules composed by children seeing the school through the eyes of their teachers (and children must see schools thus on occasion, or teachers' lives will become intolerable). On the other hand, in rules like 'Don't...Push, kick, nip, smack' and 'Don't...Chase anyone unless they want to be chased' we catch a glimpse of the schoolyard as it is for the suddenly oppressed. And in 'Do...Keep your saliva to yourself' we see a happy combination of the child's fear of being spat at and the teacher's propriety: saliva, not spit. Through all this we can glimpse an authentic, negotiated, semi-legal system.

The Barnsley Profile places the school in its society. Sue Mulvaney explained to me how everything we do as teachers is related to the environment; that to know a school you have to know about the place where it is. To another headteacher, the setting was irrelevant. 'What do you want to know about all that for?' Indeed, some powerful schools effectively cut themselves off from their environment: 'I don't care what the government says. I've got my parents and my governors with me, my test results are OK'. That was the headteacher of what I have caricatured in my introduction as a 'hessian and teazle single party state'. Such schools give the impression of being states that have made unilateral declarations of independence from their local authorities, and which survive, nourished (if that is the right word) by the charisma of the headteacher and the discipleship of the rest of the staff.

The flag is an appropriate image to fly here. Some school-states have free trade and open border posts; they are multi-lingual in all sorts of ways, and travellers, tourists, journalists are welcome. You never feel in these schools that some senior government official is listening to everything you say. Other schools protect their trade, their intellectual ideas, and shield themselves from the influence of other teachers. They put up high borders, stamp your passport on entry and, though they may well be multi-lingual in a literal sense ('There are Bengalis, Sikhs, English and a German family here' said the headteacher of one of the UDI schools referred to above), there is only one educational language spoken. It is the language of the school's central government, and travellers and tourists are either not welcome at all or journey under serious restrictions.

Words are all we have: Holdbrook JMI, Hertfordshire

There is a reproduction on the wall of the headteacher Alan Parkinson's room. A small boy wearing dungarees holds a book on his knee, and looks out over a tenement block, similar in some ways to the flats that surround this school. All around the room is the apparatus of the modern headteacher: curriculum guidelines, a Personnel Guide, National Curriculum files, a Primary Teacher's Resource Pack. On the floor is a guitar, which, with the little boy, seems to be at the centre of things, and over the desk has been roughly stuck a piece of work by a young child. It is easy to imagine the conversation: Mr Parkinson, do look at what Anne's done today...That is really lovely, Anne, can you tell me about it?...I would very much like to have your work in my room ...Is that all right? Can I take it?...I'll stick it here, look...thank you very much indeed...

> We've based our PSE on the work of Chris Watkins at the Institute of Education at London University, the seven expanded selves: bodily, sexual, social, vocational, moral/political, self as a learner and self in the organisation...[see Introduction]. We fleshed that out in lots of staff meetings to see what it meant for us, where we could actually bring each of these things into practice, and then extending it, the mathematical, the scientific, the artistic self, and we're at that stage now where we're saying, "what does a mathematician, a scientist, an artist do...?", hampered and harassed as we are, of course, by the present National Curriculum...

I suspect Alan overstates this slightly, as one does when one feels oppressed. Later, the deputy headteacher, Annabelle Dixon, puts it differently: 'We try not to let our curriculum be constrained by the National Curriculum...We were encouraged by what someone, was it Duncan Graham?, said early on about the National Curriculum not being the only one...'

Alan continued:

When we did this looking at the selves...we looked at the headings that were there and said where shall we start, social selves, we were just opening the file at random, social selves, communicating with family and friends in community and receiving feedback, where does this happen in school?

So as a staff we asked: where we might be doing this? At a simple level, taking and bringing messages...talking in class in group situations...teachers listening to children and expecting an answer, taking criticism, working together for assemblies, this all still needs to be written up. That was our way of saying where we're putting PSE in at present...we haven't got to the stage ('Thank Heaven!', said Annabelle later) of saying Thursday afternoons, this is PSE...

We actually do a lot of work on the central concepts: working in groups, problem-solving, an essential part of what we're doing all the time. We have assemblies where the children do them...three weeks ago, two seven year olds produced an assembly, organised the rest of the class, got them into groups...

As I redraft this chapter (April 1994) the rhetoric of the bland voice at the centre, the plain, phonily blunt politician, is all about 'the basics', though the meaning of that word is subjected to often intemperate debate. While for conservative politicians and educators 'the basics' consist of grammar, arithmetic and the simple distinction between right and wrong, for Alan Parkinson they are working in groups and problem-solving. Or, to choose an example from another school, long ago and quite far away, when a child writes

my sister said does that mean she's gonna die and I sat there and cried my eyes out I was so shocked, and the doctors and nurses were really nice they were crying to because they thought she was so buitiful

(see chapter 2) is it more 'basic' to correct spelling or to share memories of the death of a baby sister? Working in groups, problem-solving, dealing with love and death – these are the 'basics', which are, above all, opportunities to learn about our own nature, and the way we relate to fellow human beings. Alan continued:

PSE is feeling you have a stake in society, isn't it? Teaching children what's right and what's wrong...[questioning look]...well, what *is* right and wrong? All our philosophy here is about starting from where the children are, what the children need to understand, to understand themselves, to understand their society...Then you can begin to tease out what is right and wrong...

This part of Alan's comments came when I put it to him that most local authorities, if they were doing anything about PSME at all, were treating it as a control system. His vision of the issues is different. The roots, for him, are downright political – that is, they are based on a democratic model:

> We have a meeting...we sit in a circle...I started it off with third and fourth years; when the school got a bit smaller, it's with all the juniors, every Wednesday. It's been very interesting. We have a chairman [sic]. It's flagging a bit, next term we'll have a bit of structure, someone'll bring something in that's prepared. We always take it seriously, bring things back to the staff...the first issue that came up was soft toilet rolls! We'd never thought of that...and that's important, nothing should be hidden, just because it feels, well, funny, or trivial...
>
> It's trying to create a sense of empowerment, that's what PSE is about, realising the places to go to be able to develop yourself and to develop yourself within the community...
>
> I think you need a framework, an individual framework for each school, each set of teachers...you set the framework by the way you set the agenda in the school, you set up a co-operative group...it's got to be a practical framework that is seen to work, if I've got no moral framework I can't do it...How a government, by the way, can bribe parents out of the state system and talk about rights and wrongs is beyond me...

Alan here raises his shoulders in a theatrical shrug. He represents a widely held view about current government policy. This is a secret from policy makers, and influential people outside education. They are simply unaware of the depths to which the credibility of government policy has sunk in the eyes of many teachers.

I asked Alan, did he use a curriculum audit:

> An audit?...No. Admittedly, we found that 'answering questions when they arise' didn't work for sex education, so you do need something like that for some things, but mostly it's covered in a moral framework...Annabelle and I had a day to thrash things out...an overlap model with the child in the middle, and around the child are all the relationships that child has got with parents and teachers, etc., in the school...language skills, because language skills help to develop relationships, without language they thump each other. Words like 'agree' and 'disagree'...we teach them to say 'I disagree with you' not 'you're wrong,' THUMP!

In the hall there is no graveyard silence as the children come into assembly. Instead, there is a quiet, social noise of words (more words – everything at Holdbrook is concerned with words and what they can do), of mutual greeting. Nobody polices the room, or walks round the back, 'riding shotgun' (as one teacher memorably, horribly, put it to me on my first day in a headship). The displays on the walls are, Alan had told me, all the children's: HOLDBROOK ART GALLERY heads a panel of paintings based on painters in National Curriculum Art. 'The displays are not so pretty as they might be' says Alan, and later Annabelle says,

> We've got some very accomplished art teachers here who could put up wonderful displays, but we feel it's more important that the children should have control...What do children learn from such glamorous presentations done by adults? There is a place for such displays as giving an example, but that should be their purpose.

I have already said something about display in the introduction, and if I'm labouring the matter here, this is because children, parents, visitors (not to mention PSME-hounds) have, inevitably, to read the signs and symbols on the walls as part of a school's experience of teaching and learning. Those frames (often frame after frame after frame) tell us, for example, that here a piece of learning has been finished. Image after image after image – derived, however distantly, from an artist perceived as great – tell us that staff in a school value received opinions above current ones, especially the opinions of the learners in the place.

I am reminded of an infant school in Sheffield. The headteacher believed in the centrality of play to learning, and eventually the staff moved to a position where many of the displays were interactive: children could play with them, manipulate them. The same principle stands at Holdbrook. The displays are run by the children. PSE (at least as conceived by teachers like Alan and Annabelle) and play have this central idea in common, that the teaching role is to provide experiences that show us the children are moving from a partial understanding to a less partial one. This role contrasts with the currently fashionable one (at least as far as policy documents are concerned), in which the teacher is really a junior Quality Control Officer managed by more senior officers. In this model play is inefficient and therefore irrelevant because, depending as it does on the child's thinking and feeling, it doesn't necessarily go where the teacher wants it to go.

There is no compulsory uniform at Holdbrook (Joan Webster, at Cavell, I note later, also felt strongly that uniform was an infringement of children's rights); and there is that working class feel: boys in Spurs football gear and track suits, girls in disco wear: short skirts, tight trousers.

'Can we come into assembly?' say two cooks to Alan. 'Course you can, you know you can'. I am sitting now at the back of the hall with my notebook. Every item in the assembly is applauded, including a seven-year-old girl's performance of 'Busy Bee', the earliest recorder exercise, which is a repeated phrase all on b natural: short short long short short long...One or two more expert recorder players look knowingly at each other during this performance. There are models, paintings, songs, and guitar duos with the visiting guitar teacher, who doubles as a session musician, he later tells me. At the end, it appears that one Year 6 girl is leaving today. Alan's speech is pure PSE in so many ways:

> I remember when she was frightened...she didn't want to be left at school...Now she is confident, and do you remember? She sang in this hall to everybody at Christmas. She has learned to stand up for herself, particularly against boys, who tend to push girls around...Laura, all the best...here's a present [a book about water colour painting] to remind you of what you learned here...

Would the Quality Control Officer/headteacher have had time to watch this development in one child, and the will to remember it? Would s/he have had the ability to say what Alan has said today?

On the way to the staffroom I notice the labels. The message is that the school's discourse contains more than one language, but I reflect that there are some multi-language schools that only tell one story. At Holdbrook, the way you talk about football, dancing, or food, and whichever language you speak, it's all going to be heard. On the clock in the hallway it says:

orologio
clock
masa saati

and on the dining room door:

dining room
yemels odasi
sala da pranzo

In the staffroom Annabelle tells me that there are Turkish and

Italian children here, and enlarges on Alan's theme about PSE being everywhere. She says something that is going to be a central part of the day: 'PSE...it's there, in the RE...with the words...'

Alan laughs at her. 'Words! Everything starts from words!' There is an air of genial banter among the staff which you often find when one teacher has a secure intellectual grasp of a concept which the rest of the staff, teachers and others, understand to a greater or lesser degree, and which they are helping to realise. 'But it does though!' says Annabelle. 'In the beginning was the Word'. They must have had this conversation so many times. Someone else asks, 'What do the Bee Gees and Ivy Compton-Burnett have in common?' and the answer emerges as the line, 'Words are all we have'. Later, while we were talking about bereavement, Alan told me how they developed their RE curriculum:

> Words being always the first way in with Annabelle, we all sit and brainstorm the words we need for it and sort them out into packages, good words, bad words. We had a list of books that dealt with that particular thing, times of sadness, for example, dealing with the hamsters going in a proper way. If it's appropriate, we discuss grandmas dying with the whole school...

In other words, when they sit down to work on curriculum issues, the teachers at this school start with almost blank sheets of paper and then fill them with relevant words. One such sheet, "Self in the Organisation", has these headings:

- to learn a new organisation
- to use organisations in a constructive way
- to be an active participant in organisations
- to access help in an organisation
- to handle transitions between organisations
- to identify opportunities and choice in an organisation

This piece of paper has been, literally, scribbled on during a staff meeting. For example, under 'active participant' it says:

> Wednesday assembly – clubs – *opportunity* to participate must be given. Displays Organisation of the classroom etc. Organisation of *their* clubs. etc. And of Wendy House clothes etc. *Power & responsibility* to and within the organisation (self-interest)

At the bottom of the page, someone has written 'semiotic-uniform/sex'

Of course, 'Wendy House' should be 'Home Corner'. But even

more disturbing than the old-fashioned sexism is the fact that, as Annabelle later tells me, 'HMIs are now saying you shouldn't have home corners'. And yet it is in these corners that genuine autonomy does sometimes arrive for the youngest children. Indeed, in classrooms like Annabelle's, children have the chance of some privacy, which is a pre-condition for self-directed learning.

Alan's honesty is evident. He says, 'I don't know' in answer to lots of questions and, when asked about racist attacks, concedes that there are more than he knows about.

> There is no easy answer in PSE...We try to see both sides of an argument...Are there some occasions when you tell lies?...Is it right to thieve sometimes, like if your family was starving?...I think we have to raise these things, not suggests everything is always cut and dried, like the Government suggests in all its pronouncements...That's the thing with PSE, there ain't no easy answers!

Was it H. L. Mencken who said that every problem has a simple solution that is wrong?

Alan lives, in his school, with Erich Fromm's 'positive freedom ...associated with rational doubt "which is rooted in the freedom of thinking and which dares to question established views"' (*The Fear of Freedom*, 1942). I ask Alan about the picture of the boy in dungarees holding a book on his knee. 'The picture was here when I came, I would never move it, it's a treasure...'

Talking to the children, I discover that much is the same as anywhere else. Matthew says Nicky pulled him down the hill, and he has just told the dinner lady. The difference is in the way the words of the children are respected. When a child shows a teacher a new piece of work, the teacher always assumes there is a story behind it, and finds time to listen to it. Anthony, in Annabelle's class, is seven and he is showing me a painting of a hill:

> Well in one of these doors there this kind of crystal and when – there's a monster near the crystal and it's guarding it and near it there's this trap door and it goes all the way down under the picture up to this bear's cave and when it gets to this bear's cave it finds this kind of bed and then he sleeps in it and when the bear comes home he eats him up!

This classroom looks cluttered, but it's a powerful clutter: old rugs, settees, storage systems, words on the wall headed 'I read the names on the register', 'I shared something with the class' and 'I chose a story'. The room, Annabelle says, is divided into 'areas of development, centres of interest'. Each of these areas is about the size of a small bathroom: one has small building materials in it, and another large building materials; here is the language area, with books, paper, pencils, typewriters, a computer with a word processor programme in it, and a tape recorder; here is mathematics, with paper and pencils, calculators, an abacus; here is music with its glockenspiels and drums and an old guitar. Much of what is here has been chosen by the children. Also, Annabelle tells me, 'I want something challenging and exciting in each of these areas'. It reminds me of a little university, a perfect arrangement for a community of scholars.

Teachers in 'hessian and teazle single party states' would be surprised at the appearance of this place. Surely children deserve quality, they would say; the room should be less full and should contain tasteful furniture, and the work on the walls should be mounted and displayed by teachers, who in some schools are practised experts in this area. In one school, when I told the headteacher I'd be talking to the children about 'drafting and re-drafting', she replied, 'I hope you're not going to do anything that goes against my handwriting policy'. But this attitude, like the displays done by staff, is what Annabelle would call 'sterile'. It is lovely when children imitate Mondrian and have their paintings triple-mounted by the teacher, each mount corresponding to a colour in the painting. Also it is lovely when writing is displayed in immaculate italic. But surely it is not so much a living education as evidence of the hegemony of a kind of middle-class, middle-brow liberalism that still survives, despite the last fifteen years and the escalating, more autocratic style we might sadly summarise in the names of successive Secretaries of State for Education.

Annabelle takes education seriously. She is writing a book ('maybe it's two books really') 'about two things – "toolwords", and having been a Froebel teacher for twenty years'. But when we talk about this over lunch, words about all sorts of other things get in the way. Eventually she tells me how it all began, at a previous school:

> What bothered me in this infant class was that children walked away from social problems – they either walked away from things or they started to get aggressive.

Cedric Cullingford, in a 1994 article in the *Cambridge Journal of Education*, 'The Attitudes of Children to their Environment', found this was the same with domestic problems: 'Children feel that the solution to all this quarrelling is to get away from it; hence the desire for their own rooms'.

Annabelle told me that it is a matter of possession:

Whatever the quarrel was about, there were certain resources, either me or another adult. They only seemed to have two strategies and, I thought, was that justifying my view of it, I wanted to confirm in my mind that that was happening

She did some action research with diary, video and radio mikes, to see if her impressions were confirmed. They were: the children either left the field, disappearing from the scene, or they fought.

I wanted to see how they saw these situations, so I said to them, it seems to me that when you have a problem you do one of two things, you either fight about it or you go away from it. Do you think there are other ways?

And that was when one of the children said to me, 'What's a problem?' Ah, I thought, if they don't know what 'problem' is, they're not recognising what the situation is when they come up against it. Each time it's a novelty, it's a novel situation. They don't think: oh, this is the same as the other one. If they're having a problem with someone, and they're also having a problem with a friend, they are separate events, not seen as something called a 'problem'.

So we talked about it, we talked about various ways in which they might solve these things called problems. And...they started coming back with what they saw as the nub of 'problems' and we started getting more and more and more as they started thinking...were there ways of sorting certain problems? And they came up...with some really inventive ideas, absolutely wonderful. One little boy in the wendy house...he was quarrelling with another one about a pair of shoes, and I went over to them to sort it out, and they said, no, *we're* going to sort this out, and when they came out, one of them had got the left shoe, and the other had got the right shoe. Only a child could see that was a viable way of solving a problem, and they were as pleased as Punch.

Annabelle reflected that if we aren't aware that children don't know what 'problem' is, what other conceptual gaps are we unaware of? By discussion, Annabelle and her class of infants 'constructed a meaning for problem. We collected problems, examples of problems. "Is this what we mean?" I asked the class, meaning all of us, "Is this what we mean by a problem?"' She wanted, she told me much later, when I had begun to absorb the values she and Alan were concerned with, to help the children to come up with shared meanings. She wanted to give children a power over words that would then give them power over what they were doing and learning.

Power? I wanted to ask. We slipped into the question of teachers' power:

> The National Curriculum has taken over the minds and judgements of teachers...They've caved in...Scared, they've let it take over. But some *are* taking it back. They've been down the road and stopped themselves...The government is taking our words away. *They've taken away our words;* ticklists have taken away our thinking, you work at home to do your work, and think, hang on, what am I doing...

This feeling of disempowerment by the imposition of clerical tasks is widespread. A newly-qualified teacher on a course on children's writing that I was leading said to me over coffee, 'I'm disillusioned...I came here wanting to work with children but I spend loads, loads of time filling in forms, not teaching. The National Curriculum has trammelled me, I'm pissed off with it'.

I asked this teacher to present her feelings to the group of thirty teachers who had signed up for my course. Several older teachers said they had gone beyond that. 'Now's the time,' one said, 'to fight for values that transcend the values of the marketplace: love, and freedom, and autonomy...It's still all up for grabs...the National Curriculum has thousands of ways in for teachers anxious to help children to collaborate...'

Annabelle's expression 'toolwords' arose again from another teacher at Holdbrook, Sam. She had only been teaching for a year and half, and she wasn't at all disillusioned: full of enthusiasm for the job she was doing, and utterly unharassed, except by the lack of heat in the building: the temperature in her room was, she said, 12 degrees. 'But, no, this school is marvellous, you can go to Alan with anything and he'll listen. I love these kids, they're so creative. I try to see what the toolwords, the keywords are, for anything I'm thinking about...' Later, I asked her class to write about the boxes in their heads, and Perry wrote 'My box is made of people It is a humen box'.

I talked again about the expression 'toolwords' to Annabelle and she said her cousin, a mathematician, had asked her, 'Do you think there are toolwords you are learning all your life?' On reflection, Annabelle thought this was so in many different areas of peoples' lives. 'Emotional blackmail' had come to her mind: it had defined something for her when she was an adolescent. As she told me this, I scrabbled around for an equivalent, and found 'moral panic', a phrase that had defined, somehow, a reactionary approach to PSME, an approach triggered by the moral behaviour of people less well-off and less powerful than ourselves. Much later, I realised that the twin terms 'crucifixion' and 'resurrection' had come to stand for, respectively, moments in my own life that were characterised by a sense of defeat, and moments that were characterized by – no, not victory: recovery. The problem with such words, I reflected later, was that they might become clichés in the contexts of our lives, templates that dictated rather than enlivened our thinking.

But I wondered then whether looking for toolwords collaboratively with a class of children might not be a way of increasing respect for each other's points of view, a way of coming to understand one another; a way (I am tempted to write 'therefore') of democratising our schools.

Annabelle had asked teachers to define toolwords in art, and they'd come up with 'processes...elements...actions...'

> I test or assess a need for a toolword by looking to see if the children have had the relevant experience but might not have learned the word that encapsulates that experience.
>
> I collected all these examples of how they were learning to solve their problems, and looking at it a year later they were so much more positive about how they went about it, they'd solved all kinds of problems...So from then on I developed the approach, and have been trying to find out what toolwords seem to be the essential words for children to make the most of their learning...There seem to be about twenty basic ones...

Annabelle didn't tell me what these words were. But then I understood it was my challenge to find them, and yours. And, after all, she must be keeping something back for her books.

What sort of country is Holdbrook? It is a genial democracy in limestone, forming 'the one landscape that we, the inconstant ones,/Are consistently homesick for...' (Auden: 'In Praise of Limestone', *Collected Poems*). Auden's metaphor is of a countryside that 'dissolves in water'. Holdbrook changes shape according to the needs of the human beings in it. It is startlingly open to the visitor: its people seem to say, having nothing to hide, 'Like you we are imperfect, but we are doing our best...'

Rising Stars: Cavell First School, Norwich

PSME is, as I have argued, an exercise in fairness and in being open, and this chapter isn't just a description of such a process. It is, or aims to be, an example. I sent the first draft of my description of Cavell First to the headteacher, and she and her staff objected to much of it. 'The first part of the chapter gives a fair and accurate snapshot of the school...As the chapter proceeded each of us was filled with consternation and dismay'. Indeed, the first part, which was largely approved by everyone, was forgotten in the comments on the last part of my script. What follows is a mixture of most of my original words, with some alterations made in terms of the teachers' criticisms, and some of those criticisms are given in full. Serious changes are clearly flagged.

A colleague told me about Cavell First School in Norwich, and after I had rung to make a date to see the school, a large envelope arrived through the post. It contained two copies of a magazine of children's work, *Rising Stars*. The first pages I looked at told parents about their children's emerging talents as writers: 'Jasmine's writing. She is 4 years old...by our reception class responding to a painting by Francis Bacon...Notice how William is aware of the initial and the final sound in several words'. Teachers at Cavell are aware that much of the whirlwind we, as teachers, have reaped over the past twenty years has been a result of our failure, lack of interest even, in telling parents the reasons we do things, let alone discussing our teaching with them.

Other pages of *Rising Stars* were full of the kind of writing that children do when they are set free to write what they want, unimpeded by what used to be called the creative writing movement, or by notions of poetry, or by other adult impositions. Almost all the contributions have the authentic smell of childhood:

One Summer Monday. Me and Carl went fishing with my grandad. We fished out a boot. In the boot was a bit of green skin. We looked at the skin it was all bumpy. My grandad said it was crokudiyls skin ...

meand James
Lfni d LT

**You and James
laugh alot! What
do you laugh about?**

meandJames
LFnl the PgD
We L abrsE Js

**Can you tell me a
joke!**

There is also evidence of how much the children like their school (though whether you'd get published in a school magazine with contrary views is another matter):

Reasons to be cheerful at Cavell...we have got nice teachers...we are lucky to be allowed to make puppets...Everyone is happy at Cavell...The library is fun...Cavell was made with a lot of thought...Cavell is superb...The school is brilliant

Later I visited the school on a cold day in December. I was there from 8.30 till 11.00 a.m. – time only for a snapshot which would be augmented with various materials from the school, including *Rising Stars* and policy statements. Joan Webster, the headteacher, had insisted I arrive before school started 'because that is a critical time for PSE'. She was right, of course – and I was able to see the school's priority in action: 'Parents are central here...My door is always open, even when I've got a visitor'. Indeed, while we were talking, a parent came in with an enquiry about school meals. Her toddler in a bright plastic mac gazed interestedly at me. I noted Joan's bright smile, her clear demonstration to this parent that she had all Mrs Webster's attention for this part of the day.

There is a notice on a classroom door which I was to see later which reads:

HELP!

We need it! Mums, Dads, Grans, Uncles, Aunts – ALL welcome to come in anytime!

and the school's statement of policy makes this priority explicit: 'We believe and acknowledge the rights of parents and families to be involved...' Outside there are parents everywhere on the verandahs that surround the two yards. And as we walk round the school later Joan has a word for nearly all of them.

Joan tells me that her interest in PSE began in 1984 when she decided to do something about the fact that the children's lunchtime behaviour was bad, 'as it is in most schools'. She joined a research group at the University of East Anglia, and from this have grown certain principles and ways of behaving in the school. (A child comes in with a Christmas card: 'Oh, thank you! That is rather early...but thank you, thank you very much'). 'We are ourselves...we cry, laugh, talk in front of the children...'

We want to teach children to think for themselves, not to be like sheep...not to be aggressive. They have only one chance in school, they are entitled to the best we can offer...I don't think they should have all their decisions made for them, so they don't wear uniform, they go to the loo when they want, they don't have to ask...They sit where they want in assembly, they have a choice of where they spend playtime, playground, library or my room...We want them to know that the answer is in your hands, it's your move...

A boy comes up to Joan in one of the cloakrooms with a frown:

'David is kicking me.'
'What,' asks Joan, 'are you going to do about it?'
'Sort it out.'
'Where?'
'In the classroom.'

This was where the first objections came. Recording events originally as baldly as this, I was trying to get a flavour of a conversation in a school about an issue – violence of however minor a kind – that is central to PSME. Often, a fact simply recorded is better than a fact recorded and then obscured by comment. Some of the staff, however, say that it 'sounds uncaring', and perhaps we need to place it in the context of the school's talk-it-out policy. So I do. This policy says:

The term 'talking out' was adopted as one that was usable, comprehensible, and acceptable to adults and children. Children were told that solving problems with any form of violence was unacceptable and would not be tolerated...and that the process of 'talking out' should take place. This involved

1. Talking to each other about the problem and *negotiating* the outcome

2. Agreeing not to engage in physical (except a kiss or cuddle!) solutions to problems...

What follows in the policy document are five ways in which adults might help children 'talk out' problems. These involve providing good examples in their own relationships; teaching children to listen and respond reasonably, agreeing a solution that is mutually acceptable; providing spaces for children to 'talk out'; providing 'back up' when children are in difficulties with this procedure; and providing opportunities for children to work together. Once again, we come across the importance of words and their contexts. In this school, time is taken to get to the root of difficulties.

In one room is a large colourful display of the Pied Piper. All the images in it are obviously the children's. This is not so common as it might be as Christmas draws near: in the same week, in another school not otherwise referred to in this book, I saw a display of the angels on the hill at Bethlehem. All the angels wore identical templated robes and wings, and demure expressions, eyes cast down, solemn mouths, obviously drawn by the teacher in case, I suppose, the children should profane this time of the year with their often hilarious images. On the Pied Piper display, there are speech bubbles coming from everybody's mouths, and the handwriting in them is the children's: 'I like the music...Bye Bye Mummy see you later...I miss my dog...Look after Milly Mum...'

The examples shown demonstrate how seriously written communication is taken, and the same is true of their talk. I note six-year-old Andrew's confidence in his writing – his attempt at difficult words, for example: 'CLF' for 'colourful', and 'DYLT' for 'delighted'; and I note also how children are taught about communication as the teachers' take the children's written comments seriously. This seriousness breeds confidence in the children which is palpable as they handle any of the many ways their work is published: on the walls, in the school magazine *Rising Stars*, in little books kept in their trays, some of which are entirely for their own use, and which the teacher may not see. Like the children at Holdbrook, these children are surrounded by words. A teacher tells me later, at coffee time, 'You have to give them a language to talk about things... '

As I make notes about the classroom, Joan is telling me about the catchment area: 'Mainly from the council estate...Eight of the staff have chosen to send their children here. Some come from B & B accommodation, some have been repossessed, some come from outside the area because they like our policy of resolving conflict by talking out...' (This is Joan's emendation to my earlier script. It doesn't ring true, though I am sure it is what she meant. She had at first talked about 'our policy of non-violence', a phrase of such frank simplicity I'd wished I had thought of it).

Five-year-old Craig is sitting in a quiet corner – school hasn't officially started yet – and he is listening to *Burglar Bill* on headphones, and following the text carefully. A child whispers something to Joan with a shy smile. 'Oh well done! I think you must stand in assembly and have a clap today!' ('This sounds condescending' a teacher comments. To me it sounds like praise pure and simple, and the sort of thing that happens in good infant schools all over the country).

Then suddenly, in one classroom, a teacher raises her right hand. Joan sees this, stops talking to me, and raises her right hand too. Gradually, one by one, two by two, in little groups, all the children notice, raise their hands and fall silent. This is, it dawns on me, a technique for getting silence in a room without shouting. The same happens next door. 'The children can do this as well,' Joan tells me later. 'It can be embarrassing in assembly if they think there's too much noise!' I regret very much not seeing this happen, as it must be dramatic to watch an assembly stalled by a determined five-year-old's raised hand, and it would be a dramatic example of child autonomy.

A beautiful scene: in a reception class, a boy and a girl are sitting on a large, elegant, white cardboard construction labelled LOOK IN OUR ICE CAVE. So I do. There is quiet music in there, coming from a tape recorder. Owen looks at me and says, 'I need a hot drink'. He rubs his hands together. Carla comes out of the cave and asks me, 'What are you writing?' I show her, conscious that I am briefly part of the school's language policy, and therefore on my mettle. I tell her I am writing a story about her school. She looks at my notebook, then back at me pointedly. So I read her some of it. 'It says "LOOK IN OUR ICE CAVE,"' I say. Then, 'I need hot blackcurrant,' Owen tells me. 'I need hot milk'. They go back in the ice cave. A display says, 'We are all Rising Stars!' The children are being directed about their potential as human beings. They are being gradually convinced of their own possible charisma. Or, as Joan's interpolated note in my first draft prefers it, 'being given a sense of self-worth'. Not a bad thing, when some schools are convincing children only of their possibility for failure. 'You,' says a teacher, wickedly, in chapter 7, 'will go to prison, young man.'

At 10.00 a.m., as I walk round the school on my own, I am reflecting on charisma. Joan's conversation is dotted with enthusiastic exclamation marks, and she seems to make things happen by force of personality.

This is where my typescript went blue. 'WHAT!!!...Rubbish!... It's teamwork and the whole staff support you [Joan]...No!... This makes it sound like a prison...a Fascist state! Dictatorial...Staff act on the basis of their own firmly held beliefs, not because of the head's charisma'. So say the staff here, in notes written on my typescript. And the suggestion that Joan works in this charismatic way was the main stumbling block as far as my original notes were concerned. It was indeed impressive how concerted the support for Joan was in the face of this perceived attack. One teacher implied that I will use this fact to reinforce Joan as autocratic.

Now, in other schools, at all levels of the system, I have seen charisma bite into, even destroy, others' autonomy. In some schools, felt tips pens are banned, and in others, teachers only hold meetings under the headteacher's powerful auspices. A headteacher in Joan's authority told me about appointments in one school being made 'on the top of a bus' (nearly everyone objected to this anecdote, although it was nothing to do with Cavell), and I can extend what he meant to other ways teachers, or heads of state, make decisions. I suppose I have a worry that charisma is a mode of control. Charismatic leaders develop clubs around them that go on to control decision-making machinery. The fluency that is one of charisma's most evident characteristics enables the charismatic leader to proceed without potential opposition. This is the picture the Cavell teachers objected to.

And yet history teaches us that change cannot happen without charisma. Here is a central paradox: often those educators who have reflected sufficiently on this subject to have noticed how fluency – one of the most prominent qualities of charisma – is often a mode of control, are themselves charismatic. I have seen vivid, fluent, exhilarating talkers and writers inveigh against one of the very qualities that has made them compulsive listening, compulsive reading. And that is the problem with any school that is vibrant and sure of itself. Someone has charisma. Charisma has unquestioned benefits as well as risks. Look at Cavell. It is a vivid example of a child-centred school, full of words, and concerned about the world immediately around the school: the parents and their conditions. This is a school certain of its aims and practice, certain of the criteria which the staff have designed. I was left with the impression of a powerful, loud school with an eloquent constitution of which the first clause is written in bold: AT THE HEART OF THE EDUCATIONAL PROCESS LIES THE CHILD AND THEN PARENTS...This is a humming, creative place where no-one could doubt who was in charge; where child-autonomy was impressed on staff, parents, visitors and (for all I knew) the local authority, like an eleventh commandment.

'This ['no-one could doubt who was in charge'] is not true,' says Joan. 'There have been many occasions when contractors, tradesmen, delivery men, new parents and so on have not realised who was in charge'. All the teachers who responded agreed with this. 'No way' was what I called 'child-autonomy' 'imposed on staff' or anyone else. Most eloquently, one teacher wrote

> I feel part of a team of people that are empowered, who constantly challenge, argue and debate, who care deeply for each other ... It would be so much easier if we were as sure as the writer portrays us. We do not want to be controllers. We do not want to be controlled. We do not choose to be controlled...

Another picked out my words 'fiefdom', 'fortress' and 'imposed', so I cut them out. They were not worth arguing for. But to ask 'Where does charisma fit in a democracy?' is central to PSME. In a dictionary, it fits alongside a definition that talks about 'the special magnetic appeal, charm or power of an individual ... that inspires popular loyalty or enthusiasm...' Joan possesses charisma. She is, as one teacher comments, 'a visionary leader who inspires others to put their trust in beliefs and travel along the same path – enables people to extend themselves...'

Another teacher at Cavell stung me by saying that I had abused the invitation extended by the school. I have given the staff time to reply, but I feel that there is a right to see a school from the point of view of people who don't work there. Not all perceptions will be the same. Oddly, no remarks of mine that were almost embarrassingly positive had any notes written by them. For example (these from my first draft):

> Almost all the contributions [to *Rising Stars*] have the authentic smell of childhood...All the images in it are obviously the children's...I note how children are taught about communication as the teachers take the children's written comments seriously. This seriousness breeds confidence in the children which is palpable as they handle any of the many ways their work is published: on the walls, in the school magazine *Rising Stars*, in little books kept in their trays, some of which are entirely for their own use, and which the teacher may not see. A glorious example of child-centred education...

'Sounds' said someone 'as if Cavell was too much for him to take on board'. It sounds to me, at times, as I redraft this chapter, as though the teachers at Cavell could only cope with what they saw as positive remarks.

Anyway, all schools that are any good are too much for a visitor to take on board. That doesn't prevent him or her burrowing a way in, and if s/he sees some things that make the insiders feel uncomfortable, no-one should be surprised. Teachers in a school have a very close-up view. Democracy and open-ness insist that the less immediate view also has a place.

'Will he say,' writes one teacher in blue pencil, to Joan: 'your "charismatic leadership" has influenced our comments?' I couldn't get this right, really. And no-one will. Truth is only there, as someone said, in the pursuit of discrepancy. 'You have a tiny snapshot of our school,' wrote another. 'It's too small to give you the whole picture'.

Yes, it is too small. But a large view entirely from the inside is too small, as well. It might even be distorted. Nevertheless, I am glad that Cavell's close-up perspective worked with my longer distance outsider's one to help to illuminate two central themes at both my case study schools. Firstly, the centrality of words: how important it is to give learners – children and adults – time and language to reflect on what they are doing and saying; time to work out for themselves ways out of problems and into fulfilment, out of little crucifixions into little resurrections. And, secondly, how vital it is to be open in our schools; not to hide behind barriers, whether those barriers are physical, professional or emotional.

CHAPTER TWO

Talking about birth and death

I grant that the tendency of the times is to exaggerate the good which teaching can do, but in trying to teach too much, in most matters, we have neglected others in respect of which a little sensible teaching would do no harm.

Samuel Butler *The Way of All Flesh*

... I have been told
Love wounds with heat, as death with cold ...

Ben Jonson

As I write this at noon on Wednesday, I am still shaking my head at news that came at nine this morning. A friend's baby son had been rushed into the local hospital and then by ambulance to Guy's in London, where he died during the night. I think now of the father, my friend, and I see him like Christ, calling, 'My God, My God, why hast thou forsaken me?'; I see the mother like Mary, weeping. And *my* mother is dying. She had a stroke last month, and, as I write, she is in St Thomas's Hospital in London ('Caring Twenty-Four Hours For The Community', it shouts in huge letters across the Thames to the Houses of Parliament, as though there was anything else it could be doing). After trivial questions about time and money spent travelling to and from London two or three times a week; after the cancellation of the holiday, there lies the massive statement that I and the other members of her family make in secret, if not aloud to each other: she is dying. Everyone else, ringing up, dropping in, or just walking along the street, represents a strange failure to respond to an event that, for us, is everything.

How did my education and my schooling teach me about this moment? How did my friend's education and schooling protect him against his even more terrible loss? I emphasise by repetition here the gap between the two concepts because only education, not schooling, can be serious enough to prepare us for death; only education can fill the place previously occupied (but now, for most people, vacated) by religion. Like religion, education necessarily has moments of reflection, of collaborative contemplation, and of action informed by such reflection, such contemplation. Schooling, on the other hand, will only, at best, familiarise us with the relevant customs and protocol, so that we have some idea of what to say, or not to say, when someone dies.

Robin, who was 12, wrote this after the death of his grandmother:

A love poem
There will never be another Grandmother
To look after me
To snuggle me up in her warm duvet
While she drinks her morning tea.

I would fetch the paper just for her
She liked the Guardian best
She had a go at the crossword
When she sat down to rest.

I broke up the dates when she made scones
She let me knead the bread
She once cooked pizza in its packet
Its a pity now she is dead.

No more watching hockey
While playing in the park
With little cousin Rachel –
That was a lark.

My blanket is all colours
Made bigger as I grew
It's the only thing I have now
Reminding me of you.

He doesn't struggle enough for rhymes here – 'park/lark' is technically a shrug of the shoulders – but he gives a real, solid presence to his feelings about the loss of his grandmother. And when your grandmother dies, you *do* shrug your shoulders occasionally.

Robin changed in his way of thinking and feeling about his grandmother, and his relationship with her, as he wrote, 'I broke up the dates when she made scones/ She let me knead the bread'. And every time he reads these words, there will be changes in his understanding of the human reality, death, that inspired the poem. This reality is not only the occasion of his grandmother's death, but also other deaths – in newspapers, on television. Then it's his closer relations' deaths. And, finally, it will be his own.

Everything is subjective. But as artists, we make objects to help us reflect on subjective realities. As W. H. Auden wrote about W. B. Yeats, dead the week in 1939 before Auden was writing, 'He became his admirers' (*Collected Poems*). In this poem of Robin's, his grandmother becomes, for a moment, the words he has used to construct this object, this poem. She also, in turn, becomes the admiration we as readers feel for her grandson's words, his accuracy, his details: *The Guardian*, the duvet, the scones, the blanket, the minor domestic disaster when the pizza was cooked in its packet. The poem objectifies, for a moment, for every reader of it, Robin's love for his grandmother.

Schools, as well as families, are from time to time bereaved. I worked in one where a seven-year-old boy suffered from a brain tumour. We watched Justin as he became ill; as he underwent treatment; as he gained weight with his doses of steroids, and as he lost his hair during chemotherapy; as, eventually, he started the heart-breaking process of coming to terms with his impending death, expressing his grief in conversation with staff. 'Are you all right, Justin?' said the secretary to him one day as he stumbled against her in the corridor. 'No – do you really expect me to be?' he replied.

The teachers in the school came to know his mother well as they shared her tragedy. But they were learning on their feet. They were not in any way prepared for what was happening. Of course, in one sense, you can't be prepared for such an event as the death of a child. But you can foster an atmosphere in which death is discussed; in which it is understood, however partially, as an event in life that we ignore to our cost. A friend, writing to me about the death of her grandmother, says, in response to an early draft of this chapter, 'We have a dangerous illusion that we are not surrounded by death...'

It is a critical part of a school's PSME curriculum to know how death should be handled. There is more to be done than merely coping with the crisis when it happens. Even more importantly, the curriculum must encourage talk about death, accepting its existence, in the middle of cheerful and not-so-cheerful life. That talk will come about in many ways, if we let it: through the children's own imaginative play; through Religious Education; in the telling of stories from all traditions; in English, as children read poetry, fiction and drama; in science, as they watch animals. If there has to be a week in the year when we talk about death, because the PSME curriculum says so, we should still be aware it is a subject for the rest of the time too.

Here we are at an extreme end of a social interactionist approach. At one end, blissful ignorance, at the other, death. Children have, perforce, to come to terms with death, but still 'to curse the day/ I became mortal the night my father died' (Dannie Abse, 'Interview with a spirit healer', *Selected Poems* 1970). Arguably the deepest tragedy is that of children who literally 'become mortal' before their parents, like Justin and – most horrifically – Jamie Bulger who, inevitably, haunts these pages. All of us travel the road that goes from total unawareness of our mortality to its decisive suddenness, and even as children we have to begin to understand what it is to relate to the facts of life and death. We start to learn what it is to be bereaved.

One hopes this learning is done first through the loss of pet animals, both at home and at school. Many of us have, as parents, watched a young child grieve for a dog or another animal. My four-year-old son had been told he couldn't pick his pet rabbit up, 'because he's too big – you might hurt him'. When the rabbit died he said, 'I never learned how to pick him up'. In this remark he gets close to acknowledging, in his sadness, that there was more learning to do. When I published, in a British anthology, (Polly Richardson's and Meg Rutherford's *Animal Poems* (1992)), a poem for my son about the death of his rabbit, the American editor refused to allow it in the Stateside edition. It 'was just too sad'. This was a squeamishness bordering on insult to the teacher and children readers. Children intuitively understand that there is learning to be done when an animal dies.

The children at Susan Isaacs' school, The Malting House, certainly knew this. Isaacs' account of the discussion following the death of a rabbit appears in her 1930 book, *Intellectual Growth in Young Children*. Here are some of the children's remarks:

> It's dead – its tummy does not move up and down now...My daddy says that if we put it onto water we will get it alive again...If it floats it's alive, if it sinks it's dead...

I wonder here if this child has seen a Baptist baptismal service, which involves total immersion, and in which we 'pass from darkness into light'. Anyway, after the rabbit was buried, one boy said, 'It's not there – it's gone up into the sky...' They wanted to dig the rabbit up, and Mrs I. said, 'Shall we see if it's there?' and also dug. 'They...were very interested to see it still there...'

I have collected reactions to this story from adults and one child. I asked, (a) what would you say if you heard children had been allowed to dig up the body of a pet rabbit to see if it had gone to heaven? and (b) should a teacher suppress news of a pet's death and replace it with a similar specimen?

Here are some responses – not, I own up, collected with any statistical regularity, but still, I suggest, telling us something about the way we react in schools and families when teachers and children confront death – even the death of a rabbit:

Mother and publisher aged about 35:
(a) I'd be shocked. Is the teacher completely stupid? [satirical imitation of child's voice] 'Granny's just died and I want to see if she's still there. Can I? Can I?' [normal voice] To plan to dig up this rabbit after a little ceremony – Christians, not just Christians, might have something to say about that. Many of the parents would be shocked, they'd take their children away...(b) Some of the children would suss out the replacement. In a home that would be awful. You've got to face up to these things. In a school, I can see that, though it might not be the best thing to do, it might be the easiest. It's what I'd probably do.

Mother and teacher aged about 48:
(a) I don't know – I wouldn't have talked about heaven – I suppose it's fair enough. I wouldn't have done it, myself. You'd have to say, we only dig up animals when I'm here, like, we don't go to graveyards and dig up bodies. You point out the health risks and all that. (b) Fair enough. It causes so much aggro, this sort of thing. You're just making Monday that bit easier. Nobody'd notice till Tuesday, anyway.

Father and educationalist, 54:
(a) My initial response to this is abhorrence. I feel really bad about it. I'm speaking as a parent and as a teacher and as a person who finds rabbits going up to heaven and all that difficult. I find it quite strange that someone would do that. But then, we answer children's questions as they arise. There is a misconception about death being dealt with. I'd be worried. I'd say, Bloody hell, I'd find that muddy carcase!' But then I'd go ahead and dig it up. (b) That's deceit. Other

teachers would leave the cage door open, and say the hamster's got out, and have 'em all looking for it, knowing it was dead. When Philip was small, I buried his white rabbit when it died, before he got up, and said, 'It's dead, I've buried it...'

Boy 12:
(a) I suppose it's good for their education but it's a bit sick. They'll find out about things, if they do go to heaven, and they'll ask a lot of questions. But it's sick because they're probably going to find a rotted animal. It's a bit horrible, I don't know why, it just is. Yes, I'd've probably liked the opportunity to dig up a dead animal when I was five. I don't know why. (b) I wouldn't like that. That's kind of lying, really, isn't it, sort of.

This echoes the concealment theme I introduced in the Introduction. The various excuses the adults used to block the children's possible learning included undefined religious qualms ('Christians, not just Christians, might have something to say about that'), health risks, a frank admission of personal feelings, possible parental reactions, and an indolent assertion that class-rooms, especially on Monday mornings, should be as easy to manage as possible. There was also a familiar reason for doing nothing that is more commonly applied to sex education – 'We answer children's questions when they arise' – almost, as Alan Parkinson fleetingly implies in chapter 1, a good reason for a cur-riculum audit. But most of us using this mantra also go home each day vaguely relieved that nothing too challenging or diffi-cult has arisen in the children's questions, whether about birth, death, sex or the meaning of the universe and everything else. This is hardly surprising, because in an environment where teachers never ask difficult questions, why should the children? Indeed, if adults rarely raise questions about these issues in their private lives, how well equipped are they to ask them in school?

But death is around children all the time. The twelve-year-old boy's comments show both the child and the adult: he would have liked the opportunity to see an animal's carcase when he was young, but it is 'a bit sick'. The adults are protecting them-selves, not the children. The boy is protecting himself. But had he had the opportunity, that he admits he would have appreciated, to dig up a carcase, he would have learned about the biology of life and death. He would be more able now to speculate on that strange discrepancy we all know, whether we admit it or not, between our disgust and our fascination with death. And, as I said at the end of chapter 1, it is through the pursuit of discrepancies, strange or not, that we learn.

Alan Parkinson, of Holdbrook JMI (again, see chapter 1), saw these questions as learning opportunities. In answer to (a) he said, 'That wouldn't worry me in the slightest. They're finding out. Now, I'm an atheist verging on agnostic, or the other way about, maybe spiritual things would get in the way for some people, but for me it's learning...' To (b) he replied, 'Not at all, no way, not never no how, it's a chance to deal with the old problem, there's no point in telling kids stories about death written by other people when they've got an opportunity like this...'

Preparation for death is no more and no less than a celebration of living. The following extract was written by a six-year-old girl. Because it was written in 1978, when as a teacher I automatically corrected spelling and grammar, I have to present it here as filtered through my (then) secretarial obsessions:

My granny's face is very rough and when I kiss her face it feels all prickly. Her eyes are greeny-blue. When I look into them she has an oldish look. She has false teeth. She wears glasses sometimes. When she walks she wobbles a bit and her hands are creased. She is always smoking. When she smokes her mouth goes all round. Her hands go a bit red, the smoke comes out of her nose...

and this is by another six-year-old:

...It is the way she knits, it is very fast. The wool gets shorter and shorter. Then there will be no wool left. The needles clatter together. She can read a book and knit at the same time...she is always talking to herself and to other people. The needles will clatter and clatter all day long. If the doorbell rings she will always finish a row...

In these pieces, we can see children observing and celebrating. They are also thinking about the end of the wobbling, the smoking, the knitting, the reading, the talking. Soon, indeed, there will be no wool left. The arts are a powerful way in which life and death can be handled in a school. One way of helping children to think about their most significant adults is to play a game called 'Mementoes'. In this game we ask children to reflect on what they feel are the most signifcant aspects of, for example, their grandparents.

This poem of mine, which is about my son, then eight years old, helped to get it started with a group of children in Norfolk:

Mementoes

There's a place
in our garden
where the lawn's worn bare
by my goalie dives

and under the settee
in the front room
there's a pile
of Asterix books

that are falling apart.
In the bathroom
there's talc
in a bear-shaped bottle;

and the kitchen cupboards
are filled with things
my parents never eat or drink:
Appletize, tomato ketchup,

Cocopops, chocolate spread.
My drawings improve
the walls of our house
everywhere:

my monsters, my elephant,
my pyramids. Photos
abound too
where my parents work.

Me on my second birthday,
me in the temple at Karnak,
making a face. Or running
after Oscar the dog...

When I sleep round Joe's
my parents look
at these things
and wish I was home

so I could ruin the lawn.
They look in my bedroom
in the morning
and say "Shall I get him now?"

Then I am a prince
welcomed back to the kingdom.

I untidy things again
and de-silence the rooms.

I asked pupils to think about what objects reminded them of an adult – a grandparent, perhaps. What's in her garden, her front room; what are her hobbies; what is her favourite meal; what things remind you of her when she isn't around; what smells do you associate with her kitchen, what sounds? The discussion here was vivid, and both particular and general as the pupils sought to think of their grandparents in terms of objects and senses. Here, of course, they are making different objects of their relationships in a quite literal way. All the pieces in this section were corrected by the children later, in pairs.

Angela (11)

The tangy aroma of
Extra Strong mints.
The deep voise of a man,
Or a purple car.
All remind me of Grandad

Anyone dieing
Or passing away
Someone having trouble walking
A man working with wood
All remind me of Grandad

The dentists
Or docktor
Or people laughing
Or mabe a little drink
All remind me of Grandad

The discussion came to a climax when one girl said, 'My Dad was a photographer, he had lots of different kinds of cameras... and we haven't cancelled his magazine yet...' Obviously the critical word was 'was'. The teacher (a supply – the class teacher was ill) and I were nonplussed. But the other children buoyed the girl up. They watched her as she talked in this semi-public setting about her bereavement, and I felt, in that highly-charged room, that all the children, as well as myself, were thinking about death. Eventually this girl wrote:

There's a magazine
that comes through the post.
Cameras anywhere,
for Dad was a cameraman.
The sight of milk
and Dad fills my thoughts.

A battered pair of Scholls
which my Dad used to wear
living in a cupboard
dark and all alone.

In another school, Alex was seven when his mother died suddenly. He never spoke about her in school and became withdrawn. A year later a visiting poet played a game called The Magic Box, which involves children writing about the nature and contents of a box in their heads (see Perry Lamprell's lines quoted at the beginning of chapter 1). Alex wrote, 'In my box are my mum's badges...' and Alex read his writing out to the class. His teacher sent the writer a note: 'That was very brave of Alex, he hasn't mentioned his mother since she died...' We needn't turn writing into rafia-work therapy in order to insist that the arts have a function in helping us (as Samuel Johnson put it) to 'enjoy and endure'. Indeed, the badges, the photography magazine, the milk, the Scholls sandals, 'the tangy aroma of extra strong mints', 'maybe a little drink' are all what T. S. Eliot called objective correlatives: ways of making public our feelings.

In the same activity in another school, Angela, who was eleven, wrote that she had 'her Uncle Terry' in her box 'who died last week'. As she read this sentence out, the colour left her face, and she cried. So did her teacher, who hugged her. The children silently looked on. A governor who was sitting at the back of the class was unimpressed. Later, he asked the visiting writer why he taught poetry, what was the point?

At the end of the lesson, Angela told her teacher, the visiting poet and the governor a poem 'we say at home':

My friend Billy
Had a ten foot willy
He showed it to the girl next door
She thought it was a snake
So she hit it with a rake
And now it's only five foot four.

The governor was unimpressed by that, as well. In two ways, the children had subverted his limited vision of the educational purpose of schooling: by understanding how to talk about death in an artistic context, and by a ribald rhyme. Angela had demonstrated once again, for those of us who still haven't noticed, that for children, the world and all the experience it offers us, from birth – through love, hate, learning, dancing, singing, mark-making, counting, measuring, competing, indecent humour – to death is a whole web which only the writers of curriculum guidelines, and those obsessed with propriety, cut apart into convenient sections.

In a school where children's feelings are respected, and where writing is a normal part of classroom life, rather than something that happens only in writing lessons, pupils will sometimes be able to express grief and tell personal, tragic stories without any stimulus from the teacher. Indeed, Robin's 'A Love Poem', quoted earlier, was written, the teacher told me, as a response to a relatively uninspired lesson on St. Valentine's Day. Robin, and the girl who wrote the next piece, show us that children can often surprise us on the days when our teaching is less inspired than usual:

I remember when my mum was rushed to hospital because she was in labour so after school me and my sister had to go to my nannas. After we had, had our tea my uncle came round and he was talking to my nanna and my nanna looked very worried and so did my uncle. I had that feeling in my stomach that something had happened it was horrible. Me and my sister got our coats on and my uncle took us to the hospital. When we got in mums room everyone looked sad, they were crying My sister wanted to go to the toilet so she went out of the room to go. I sat on the bed and my dad said to me Charlotte hasn't got that long now and my sister said does that mean she's gonna die and I sat there and cried my eyes out I was so shocked, and the doctors and nurses were really nice they were crying to because they thought she was so buitiful. A man at the hospital took some photos of her for us. They are really lovely. Soon the doctors and nurses took her off the life suport machine and we were all aloud to hold her knowing that she had at least a little while to live it was really nice to hold her. While we were holding her she was going different colours because she was dying. While I was holding her a teardrop fell on her head and I kissed her.

The girl was laughing and playing in the playground five minutes later, as two or three teachers tried to suppress tears in the staffroom. The secretarial activity of correcting the text would have been – I've searched and searched for the correct word – *indecent* here. The one-paragraph structure represents the way in which the writer needs to pour out the story. It's a bit like the last pages of *Ulysses*, where Joyce's continuous prose portrays a woman in bed remembering and reflecting. Here, this child evokes the panic: you want to know this is how it was: 'my eyes have seen,' as Robert Lowell put it, 'what my hand did'.

In grammatical terms, it is impressive that in a first draft of a piece of writing about such a highly-charged subject, 'labour', 'stomach' and 'horrible' are correctly spelt, and any mechanistic assessment procedure would have to take account of the fact that these words were got right under this kind of pressure. The misspelling of 'allowed' is positively Joycean in its appropriateness. The child knows 'had had' (line 3) is correct to her sense, but has to put the comma there to convince herself she can get away with it. The local (Ipswich) speech is written as it is spoken ('gonna', 'buitiful'), and pronouncements from central government suggesting that this should be corrected raise issues of snobbery and racism. To discountenance local speech is a class- and race-oriented attack on children's autonomy, because it disallows and devalues something central to us all, our language. And, as Annabelle Dixon is fond of quoting (see chapter 1), 'In the beginning was the word'. Words are all we have to make us certain of our humanity.

A sound PSME curriculum will find ways of enabling pupils to express their sense of loss. It will also enable them to subvert the most sombre moments, to collapse them in laughter. It will teach children about death.

Just a moment ago my friend John told me that his mother's last words, as he tucked her in when she lay dying of cancer, were: 'You're not doing it right'. He laughed and told me that if she'd said anything else he would have been worried. What is it that helps us face up to the truth about each other and our personalities at moments like this? How do we educate children in confronting those moments?

One way is through fiction. John Burningham's *Grandpa* is too well known to need further discussion here. Alice Walker's *To Hell with Dying* (originally published in a collection of short stories called *In love and trouble*, 1967, and then re-issued with vivid illustrations by Catherine Deeter in an edition for children by Hodder and Stoughton in 1988) begins with an uncompromising sentence: 'Mr Sweet was a diabetic and an alcoholic and a guitar player and lived down the road from us on a neglected cotton farm'. This story is about the times Mr Sweet nearly dies. But, while the children are still young, he always recovers, through the agency of their at least half-deceived but still unsentimental love. 'His ability to be drunk and sober at the same time made him an ideal playmate, for he was as weak as we were and we could usually best him in wrestling...'

The issues in this book would make up a large part of a contents page for a PSME syllabus: racism, family life (Mr Sweet 'was not sure that Joe Lee...was his baby'), alcoholism, friendship, death...Each time the old man has an attack, the children's father says, 'To hell with dying, man, these children want Mr Sweet'. Indeed, Mr Sweet survives till his ninetieth birthday, when the speaker is called home from college where she is 'finishing [her] doctorate':

> I bent down and gently stroked the closed eyes and gradually they began to open. The closed wine-stained lips twitched a little, then parted in a warm, slightly embarrassed smile...

and of course, at last, he dies. This is a book that takes risks, and achieves far more than most books on this subject. It is honest, but also manages the nervy, tense optimism we need in the face of passages in our lives when we confront the possibility, and eventually the inevitablility, of death.

Sex and birth

But to 'sex' and 'birth'. Not just 'families', not just 'reproduction'. Not just 2.4 children, but also no children at all. Indeed, this area tingles with word problems. Like Annabelle's children in chapter 1, we seem at times not to have the words we need to deal with issues central to our lives and learning. One school I know has opted for the word 'beginnings' for its work on sex education, but this implies birth. And all the sex education I've been party to over the years has largely ignored aspects of sex that puritans might call hedonistic: the delight, the discovery, the changeability, what Germaine Greer called in a *Guardian* article (4 April 1994) the 'protean' nature of sex, that makes each generation discover for itself something new.

In popular usage the word 'moral' in the title of this book might seem to refer exclusively to sexual morals. J. H. Simpson, a pupil at Rugby at the beginning of the century, is quoted by

Nicholas Bagnall in *The Independent on Sunday* (12 December 1993) as saying that in his schooldays 'immorality' meant 'only one thing'. Bagnall comments, 'One imagines dire warnings being given, but since the staff felt it improper to mention sex, a euphemism was necessary'. And that euphemism was 'immorality'.

The reverberations of 'moral' are far narrower to us today than they were to Swift, who says somewhere that the English are more corrupt in their morals than any other nation. He was not, in particular, referring to sex. Aristotle's definition was even wider: 'moral excellence or virtue has to do with feelings and actions'. But we, living in the late twentieth century, cannot imagine a car thief or a fraudster being described as immoral in a newspaper; the word is reserved for sexual crimes. Even serious moral failures, like cover-ups of political scandals, are less readily referred to in moral terms than other scandals that involved what the press sees as sexual misbehaviour. (One headteacher went further and linked the word 'moral' exclusively to the notion of Christianity, unaware how offensive this was to non-believers like Alan Parkinson, and people of other religions. Also, how daft it is to anyone concerned about ensuring that education has any relationship at all, however tenuous, with justice. This constituency would, of course, include all children who use the expression, 'It isn't fair').

The anxiety is still with us today. When we say 'immoral' we usually mean 'sexually immoral'. Our own schooling and upbringing have led most of us to place the lexicon of sexual behaviour somewhere on a continuum ranging from the mildly embarrassing, through the acutely irritating, to the downright offensive. We have had little education on the subject, and the fact that we can find few teachers discussing sex adequately, let alone creatively, surely suggests we are little better now than we were at articulating this area of our experience, especially with children. One teacher told me that the only time he used the words for the genitals was when he went through his annual 'stint' of sex education videos with his year 6 class, and he did not find it easy. Traditionally, as parents, many of us have concealed sexual facts behind lies about storks and gooseberry bushes, and allowed our children to pick up other falsehoods from the playground or from television and popular culture.

I spoke to a teacher in a school that had been recommended to me as working imaginatively in this field:

> We breed guinea pigs with the youngest ones...The children look after them, care for them...I pick them up and said, look, a penis, that is a penis...we've done all the plumbing...We're not doing sex education this term, and you are looking at it in the wrong way...it's about relationships ...

I asked here, crossly and therefore mischievously, 'What do you mean? How did the children look at the relationships between the guinea pigs?' 'You are looking at it the wrong way round,' I was told again. 'We are looking after animals, and sex education is first of all about looking after each other... '

Perhaps, of course, it should be. But to dismiss the physiology of sex as 'plumbing' is to sell children (and, come to that, sex) puritanically short. And to insist that we concentrate on 'relationships' is to beg a set of serious and urgent questions. Where, in our school policies, is the sense of delight in sex? When we talk of relationships, relationships between whom? Should each generation dictate to the next what its sexual behaviour should be?

Of course, we focus much of our teaching, in one way or another, on how we relate to each other in sexual and other contexts. However, children are also interested, at a very early age, in their own bodies (as opposed to animals' bodies) and how they function, just as they are interested in the other big guns of a humane curriculum, death and violence and injustice. Also, excessive use of animals in this context sanitises the subject and, indeed, removes all the relationship aspects except feeding and physical care. It is hard to have a row with, or laugh alongside, a guinea pig, or conceive of a relationship with a tortoise that makes us rejoice one day, feel guilty the next and cry the day after.

Sue Mulvaney, headteacher of Kexborough County Primary School in Barnsley (see chapter 1), told me that sex education had a prominent place in her school:

> We give the children a freedom to see connections between topics and materials outside the traditional curriculum. Each unit has a two-year plan, we look at what we are doing and tweak it towards sex education. We have a hatchery in the nursery and reception classes, then in year 6 we jiggle classes up and another teacher and I take them in groups of about ten, we make the environment comfortable, cushions and all that, and we get down to the nitty-gritty...

I asked Sue what she thought about sex education schemes that claimed to 'answer questions when they arise'. She has a blunt way of speaking:

> Rubbish. It's a cop-out. We give them books, videos, written-down details, we allow non-attributable questions, we allow an environment for the questions to arise...One of the teachers had a baby and the questions were great, there was no dishonour, nothing was abused, it was fine. They all had biscuits and pop and they asked basic questions.

The following list tells us about the obsessions, interests and misconceptions of a group of year six children at Kexborough School, where the teachers, over a long period, encourage questions about sex. I print it in the random order in which the questions were presented at the school. I have corrected spelling, because to leave some of the wrong spellings seemed patronising, as if we expected to see the ways these children wrote about these issues as somehow quaint. I have numbered them to make reference easier:

1 What are the signs of starting your periods?
2 What is a nipple?
3 What are stretch marks?
4 Why is it that sometimes the mother dies in childbirth?
5 If you are gay do you have to use a condom?
6 How come your tunnel doesn't stretch before you have a baby? (I thought it stretched with you growing up).
7 What are pubic hairs?
8 How do you know if you've got AIDS?
9 How does a man know whether say if they wanted twins, how does he know whether he has sent like two sperms in?
10 How does the male seed get inside his body?
11 If you had sex and got pregnant then if you had sex again would it mean you would have twins?
12 What does having it off mean?
13 What causes a miscarriage?
14 How old do you have to be until your vaginal opening is big enough for you to have a baby?
15 How long does it take to make a baby?
16 Where does the milk come from?
17 Why does sometimes the baby come out when they aren't ready?

18 Can you go swimming when you are wearing a pad, it might get wet?

19 If someone has a child and they have a baby can you get AIDS?

20 How does the stomach swell up on a female?

21 Do you usually start your periods just before your mum started?

22 Why do women have babies not men?

23 Why are babies smaller if they're more of them, eg twins are bigger than triplets?

24 If the female is pregnant and he or she didn't know what will happen to the baby if they have sex again?

25 Is the baby closer to the father or the mother?

26 What are sex organs?

27 If the woman was pregnant and the woman didn't know what would happen if they had sex again?

28 Why do we grow hairs around our penis or vagina? What are they called?

29 On some tv programmes when two people are making love they make noises. Why is that?

30 Why do people poop? Why do people go to the toilet?

31 How do women's breasts produce milk?

32 When a baby is born why are there some spastics?

33 Why are people fat? Why do people grow? Why do people fight? Why do people steal? Why do people kill? What goes through their minds?

34 Why do men need condoms?

35 Why do you get Siamese twins?

36 What happens if a woman gets cancer? Does the baby get it?

By my careful but perhaps still faulty reckoning, there are six kinds of question here. This demonstrates how wide the range of knowledge and experience is in any group of ten-year-old children talking about sex and birth. The first kind of question requires basic information at a fairly low level (2, 3, 7, 10, 18, 20, 26). The second asks for information at a more advanced level, and some of these questions are informed by a kind of anxiety (1, 5, 6, 8, 14, 16, 21, 23, 28, 29, 31, 34). The third batch of questions reflects serious worries (4, 13, 17, 32, 35, 36). The fourth exposes grave misunderstandings (though I am not suggesting these misunderstandings aren't evidence of anxiety) (9, 11, 15, 19, 24). Two questions, 12 and 30, reflect playground discourse, and the frequent confusion of the sexual and the excretory. Both are, of course, taboo subjects, and also, probably, evidence of anxiety.

Finally, there are three questions – 22, 25 and 33 – which I call 'meaning-of-life questions'. Here there is more anxiety than in the group of questions I have labelled as chiefly concerned with anxiety. 'Why are people fat? Why do people grow? Why do people fight? Why do people steal? Why do people kill? What goes through their minds?' This question shows that a child has a wider and richer definition of 'moral' than many adults, and also that she has related sex education to the broad context not only of her own life, but to the world's. The question, 'Is the baby closer to the father or the mother?' places, in ten simple words, the whole debate in the difficult context of family love, where successive governments insist they want it placed.

The discussion with the teachers that follows these questions has several vital functions: it provides factual information, it comforts and allays fear, it corrects the often gross misunderstandings of a playground sub-culture, and helps children to reflect collaboratively on issues that will concern them all their lives: not just sex and love and birth, but violence (see 29 for an interesting variation on this), abnormality and disease. It also induces learning, as the process of writing down the questions is a pedagogic one. Reflect, for a moment, upon what the writer was thinking as s/he wrote, 'If the woman was pregnant and the woman didn't know what would happen if they had sex again?'

I watched my godson, seven-month-old James, being bathed by his mother, Jacquie Knott, at Sprites Junior School in Ipswich, where his father, Simon, is a teacher. The year six class had just seen a BBC video on sex education, containing film of a birth, and when Jacquie, James and I arrived, the room was still semi-dark. The children were arranged for watching the television, and now mother and child took the place of the screen. James beamed at them. They laughed delightedly back. There was no need to ask for quiet: babies seem to have a civilising influence. The children knew he would be frightened by loud sudden noises, and therefore they didn't make any. They watched intently as Jacquie undressed her baby. Then there were little whispered comments all around the room, and tiny, private conversations. This was where some of the learning was going on, as they commented on the baby to each other, and compared their perceptions with their friends'. 'In't 'e sweet,' someone said, in the local voice, without a question mark. I felt sure that these moments were as valuable as the information-giving moments, crucial as such information is. I also reflected on what learning we prevent when we stop children whispering.

James chortled and sucked his hand, and beamed when they laughed. The headteacher, Peter, sensitively elicited facts from Jacquie, about, for example, James sitting up and falling over, about how quickly babies get cold, and about his sensitive skin. Once in the bath, James delighted us all by slapping his hands on the surface of the water. Then he turned and waved at the front row. What must it all have looked like from his point of view?

Eventually, a boy raised his hand: 'Is he getting eager to walk?' Then other questions came. Being public, of course, they were different from the questions at Kexborough. Most, at first, were from boys, while the girls seemed to prefer to watch. Jacquie put bubbles in the bath, and poured water over James's hair. 'Before I had James, I'd never bathed a baby,' she said. The questions kept coming:

Does he like his toys or does he go after something else? Does he eat those tin foods? Does he wake you up much in the night? Has his pressure point gone yet?

At this point, Jacquie asked Victoria, who had put the last question, to come and feel James's head, and she and Peter talked about the fontanelle, and the bones knitting gradually together. Now dressed, James picked at a bit of paper stuck to the desk on which he was sitting, or played with a plastic transparent ball that kept falling on the floor. Peter said, 'Any other questions?' – and there were:

How much did he weigh when he was born? Is he sick a lot? What time was he born at? How long were you in labour?

It was at this point that the questions changed in character, because Jacquie told them about her Caesarean section. She said later, 'Several of the girls grimaced, and I said it wasn't that bad'. She'd started to explain what had happened. A boy said, 'They put a needle in your spine'. 'That's right,' said Jacquie. There was a quiet. As Jacquie remarked to me going home in the car, at this point more serious questions and remarks became 'legal'.

Does he get lots of feeds in the night? Did he go in an incubator? So he didn't get jaundiced? How long did he stay in the hospital? What ward was he born in? I was born in Orwell. I was born [Victoria said] in my mum's bed. My cousin was born in the ambulance on the way to the hospital. When my brother was born my mother lost a lot of blood. Do you want another one?

The questions came quicker and quicker as it was time to finish. Peter knelt down to mop the soapy water up with old newspapers.

I had driven Jacquie and James to the school, and on the way home Jacquie told me about the women she worked with who use services for people with learning difficulties. She'd realised how sheltered their lives were: 'Their ignorance of basic human activities...' One, for example, had not heard about breastfeeding. 'Why is he doing that?' she'd asked, when she'd seen Jacquie feeding James. Further, all the women had been protected, Jacquie felt, from any talk about death. 'It's the same thing as at the other end of life, the first funeral is often their parent's...those girls at Sprites had had far more experience, at least about babies, than those women had had, they'd bathed babies at least, some of these women had never even held a baby!'

One of the girls, whose mother had lost blood, had talked to Jacquie later. 'She just wanted to talk about it...she told me the story again really, then she said, "I'm the oldest of five...and my mum's 25!"'

Immediately after the birth of Jacquie's and Simon's son James, my twelve-year-old son Daniel had held him. He'd stroked his arms and legs quite unselfconsciously, and held his red feet. Then he wrote (spelling self-corrected):

Your skin is wrinkly
and soft as new cotton wool.
You moan and whinge for food.
Your mother watches you
pass between visitors.
She has a permanent loving smile.
Fondly she kisses your forehead.
You look up to her and yawn.
Your father holds you
firmly and carefully
as he would
a delicate, fragile egg.
He is thinking

'This is what we've waited for'
Your hiccuping little squeaks
shake your whole body.
Visitors laugh.
You, not seeing the joke,
hiccup again
and look annoyed.

(privately published in *Sight of the Road Home,* ed. Simon Knott, Ipswich 1993)

None of this discussion of the extremes of human experience should blind us to the fact that children face more everyday, but still terrible, crises, with which we must help them deal. I have discussed before Wes Magee's poem 'Good Questions, Bad Answers' from *Island of the children,* edited by Angela Huth (see my book *The Expressive Arts,* 1993, in this series, pp. 31–32). Ten-year-old Elly Denison listened to this poem, but subverted Magee's original nostalgic purpose (and her teacher's similar intentions) when she wrote her version (see p.59).

This poem bears careful examination (probably more careful than I, given my pressing deadline, can give it). Elly had an accident on her bike, and must have initially dealt with her broken arm by herself. She'd called on her doctor, but had got no answer, and had walked home, leaving her bike in the ditch. Let's look at the evidence of different kinds of learning we can identify in this writing, remembering that there will be many elements of learning which we can't see. First she has used the form of Magee's poem, and altered it for her own vital purposes. Magee's form is identifiable from the following poem by another ten-year-old, Helen, quoted in *The Expressive Arts,*

Where is the age of nine gone which somehow I enjoyed being? Down the drain forever.

Where are the shoes with black soles and red bows which I had three years ago? They them away.

Elly has taken this format and changed its purpose. She has accepted a real poem by a real poet, read to her by a real teacher (note all the power there, in the word 'real'); been impressed by it, and then has remembered (though at what point did this happen?) a personal crisis. She's altered the poem, and made it her own in terms of this crisis. She has operated on the world, and she has transformed it. And she has done all this in the space of an hour.

memories   name ELLy Denison   age 10

1. Wheres my bike
   In the dish

2. Where,s my doctor
   gone out

3. Where,s my home
   up the road

4. We'res my dad
   at home

5. Where,s the hospita
   In Ipswish

6. Where,s my mum
   they she is

7. Where,s my bed
   in the other ward

8. where,s the churld ward
   they ib is

9. Where,s my plaster for my arm
   naw coming

10. my arm ishurtag me
    naw coming

11. thingk you

Secondly, the spelling and the grammar. Elly makes loyal attempts at what someone has told her matters more than anything: the apostrophe in 'Where's', for example. But her significant learning – about what it was like to be injured and alone (and, by extension, about what it will be like next time, whether for herself, or for someone else) goes far beyond SAT-oriented anxiety about inverted commas and spelling. And we note, too, how she can express that learning. This is back to basics, and seriously so.

Thirdly, Elly has used the local dialect in her writing ('now coming...now coming'). Should this be stigmatised as non-standard English? Or should Elly be congratulated on her integration of this phrase in a piece of writing asked for in a lesson using standard English? Indeed this phrase is repeated, reflecting as far as one reader familiar with this dialect is concerned, the panic, the impatience, the pain. 'Don't worry,' Elly's mother must have said. 'He's now coming'.

Finally, look at the lovely relief in the number 11. Would any teacher sensitive to this account of Elly's adventure correct that? Here, and in the rest of the poem, we have evidence of Elly's learning about other people – in particular, how they exist even when one is in awful pain.

Postscript

My mother died. Some weeks after her funeral, I had just got up from my desk to wander round the house and gather breath for a new paragraph of this chapter – to make, possibly, a cup of coffee – when I wandered into my 12-year-old son's room. On his desk was a spiral notebook, and on the exposed page I read

I saw in her eyes
a smile
I was sure she was
trying her best
her right hand puffed
out of size
her right was dead
her left hand
gripped my right
And at that moment
I saw what she had
been trying to do
a huge toothy grin
her teeth were out of line
It was one of the happiest
moments of my life
but it was also one of the saddest.
17 days later she died.

CHAPTER THREE

Jumping the steps: the child's point of view

LADY CHILTERN: We were at school together, Mrs Cheveley.
MRS CHEVELEY:...Indeed! I have forgotten all about my schooldays. I have a vague impression that they were detestable.

Oscar Wilde, *An Ideal Husband*

When I get out of here, out of nursery, I'm going to say 'fart'

child in nursery

In a recent paper I've already mentioned, Cedric Cullingford analyses interviews with eight-year-old children talking about their environment. The children's comments, predictably, are illuminating and earthy, expansive and candid. On teachers, for example, someone says, 'They don't get very well paid, with all their sixty-year-old minis...' Being rich is 'blowing my nose on five pound notes...driving a Range Rover with six disc drives built in one...' Occasionally we get a glimpse into lives that sound, to use Mrs Cheveley's word, 'detestable'. For example, very few adults could respond as this next child does, and if they did they would be classified as neurotic and self-pitying. It is considered, in our culture and at our time, correct and normal to conceal these feelings, these reflections on ourselves. Children, on the other hand, tend to be more honest:

I don't like myself because I'm not very good at Maths. I'm not sure what divide and times means. I just wish I was somebody else...rich...

Another child says:

I don't like this voice really. It's a bit, um, dim. And I don't like my name.
My friend's voice...they're nice and soft and that. But mine isn't. Mine's
kind of rough. I don't like my hair, because it always gets knotty and I'd
rather like it like my friend Laura's because it never gets knotty. It's nice
and blonde. But mine's getting brown now...

Work like Cullingford's helps to see inside the dark box containing a child's feelings. It helps us test assumptions, often about
innocence. But responses like these are only possible when the
interviewer is interested in children and their views. S/he must
be prepared to express that interest, not just in articulate questioning, but also in patience, and in the art into which imagination will transform such questioning, such patience. All too often,
children are used to having their comments brushed aside or
patronised. 'Off you go, now, and fight your own battles...' 'I'm
sure Jenny didn't say that. Perhaps if you say you're sorry...'

By contrast, see how the staffs at Cavell, Holdbrook and
Kexborough Primary treat what children say (chapters 1 and 2).
In such schools there is an attempt to take every comment,
whether fictional, autobiographical or scientific, seriously. 'When
I get out of here, out of nursery, I'm going to say "fart",' said a
child to his teacher. What do we do? Usually we ignore this kind
of stuff. The ostrich position is second nature to some teachers.
We filter out all the difficult bits, or mop them up with Kleenex.
And few teacher-trainers or INSET providers that I have come
across offer much advice about a better way to deal with children's talk when it nudges up against conventional propriety.

Liz Waterland, in *Not a perfect offering* (1994), presents a fictionalised account of a girl beginning school. Art, as Picasso said, is a
lie told to tell the truth. Here that lie opens many possibilities for
those of us anxious to understand more of what a journalist
might call the child's angle on her first day at school. What is that
day like? Perhaps the teacher as artist/researcher will tell us
something we either didn't know before, or knew but didn't want
to say too much about:

She had come in the door and there was a lady that mummy said she had
seen before but there had been a fluffy dog then and he wasn't there now.
She couldn't remember the lady but she remembered the door and the
way it closed behind her very slowly as if a person you couldn't see was
shutting it with a click behind you. It had made her jump again, that little
secret click. She walked along a long carpet with little squares, one foot in

each square until she bumped into a table. Mummy tapped her head and said, 'Look where you're going'. How did she know where she was going? ...Near the door was a toy cooker...Rebecca put her hand out and touched the knob...She opened the oven door and looked in. There was a dolly inside. Why was the dolly in the oven?

I am reminded of how, in moments of crisis – a family argument, hearing of the death of a friend or relative – I notice patterns on walls and floors, as though those patterns might give shape to the experience I am currently experiencing as shapeless. In church, a two-year-old girl I don't know wanders down the aisles, treading on the maroon tiles and avoiding the ones that are yellow, as if in a private prayer of her own.

In Liz Waterland's book, a child falls over, spoiling her new coat:

If you rub the mud with your hanky it just gets more and the dirty spreads and then your hanky is dirty, too. You want to go home. You want to go home. The lady, the tall one, bends down and takes the coat away. Your hanky wipes your eyes and then someone says now it's all over your face, too...My coat, my coat, my coat. And then suddenly, there's blood hurting somewhere ...

There is something in this writing that reminds me of the beginning of Joyce's *Portrait of the Artist as a Young Man:*

When you wet the bed first it is warm then it gets cold. His mother put on the oilsheet. That had the queer smell...

and also of Picasso's remark about the need to draw 'like a child', and indeed his practice (and Klee's) of doing so. One of the achievements of the Modernists lies in attempts by artists like Joyce, Klee, Miro and Orff to see the world as a child sees it, or at least to take into account, in Orff's case, the musical education of the young in composition. Educators might attempt a similar leap in order to make schools more humane places.

Why is there no modernist literature/art written for children? Information about how children behave in our fragmented times can only be found in the sterile garden of behaviourist psychology, and about how they think in books like Donaldson's excellent but essentially non-artistic text *Children's Minds.* And such books are, of course, written exclusively for adults. Illustrators like Ardizzone, admirable as they are, rarely depict the splintering of what it is to be a human being in the twentieth century, whether that human being is child or adult. And there is a way in which that splintering is more closely focussed through the eyes of a child. But poets like de la Mare wrote as though there had been no heap of broken images to try to come to terms with, no Pound or Eliot, no *holocaust*. Dennis Lee's *Jelly Belly* (Blackie 1983), while concerned with modern issues about conflict, rage and love, is entirely written in traditional forms.

Modernist artists participated in a determined attempt to 'make it new'. They looked into the dark of the future and, while being steeped in tradition – in Eliot's case, for example, Elizabethan drama, Sanskrit, Frazer's *The Golden Bough*, classical literature and history – they were interested not only in that known body of work: they examined the dimly glimpsed, and made what Froebel called 'surmises': they developed the ability to probe into the dark, not just to rely on previous knowledge.

In her way, Waterland has got as close to achieving a child's perspective on this patchwork we call school as anyone. The rest of us – like Cullingford – have occasional glimpses into this perception if we are attentive. My son, for example, a year after he started school, was asked, just as nearly every child has been asked a thousand times, 'What did you do in school today?'

Jumping the steps, I did jumping the steps...there's these big steps and you stand at the bottom and you have to jump to the top...Sometimes Craig and me, we jump the steps, sometimes I do it on my own. Today I did it on my own...

Look again at what Waterland's little girl said: '...there had been a fluffy dog then and he wasn't there now'; '...the door and the way it closed behind her very slowly as if a person you couldn't see was shutting it with a click behind you'. If we are to see the school from a child's point of view, we might as well start from an early memory of our own about school; being told (to take real examples from colleagues' recollections) that you are to join a house tomorrow, while you're more than content with the house you live in now, with your parents, your brothers and sisters, your teddy bears; wondering why the door had 'door' on it, when you knew it was a door; wondering why the teacher's nails were red, when mummy's nails were never red.

If we are to understand PSME, we might try to appreciate the children's perspectives on their school. Indeed, we are not used to seeing school as viewable in different ways at all. We see it as an objective reality, simply there, to be dealt with by all of us as best we can. But a hospital ward is a very different place to, in turn, the child just brought in with a broken arm (see Elly Denison's poem in chapter 2); her parents; the harassed nurse just about to go off duty; the staff nurse; the doctor in her first job; the cleaner in the corridor. To the first three of these characters, the place represents nothing less than a crisis, but to each of them a different sort of crisis. To others, it represents, possibly, a bore, a worry, a challenge. Similarly, the school in Ipswich looks very different from the headteacher's room compared with how it looks from the desk where the new child from Sunderland has just started, and there is an infinite number of points in between these two, as well as possibly a few outside them. The teacher, of course, has another perspective altogether. Again, as I have shown in chapter 1, a school looks very different, from the point of view of a united staff on the inside, compared with the view of a detached outsider.

Paul Merton, the comedian, recalled on Desert Island Discs how, encouraged by a teacher, he wrote a weekly diary at school, using it as a medium for imaginative writing. When he got a new teacher, he was punished for it by having to read his diary to the class. This backfired because, rather than finding him ridiculous, the other children began to write their diaries in the same way, and the teacher had an outbreak of creative writing when she had expected the more usual accounts of the weekend. There are two lessons here. The first is that it matters to children when they find that a new teacher has a new view on things, a different one from the previous teacher. The second is that strategies developed by children to learn about themselves – whether through writing, art, conversation or other means – will not always be encouraged by a teacher who is concerned with other, more prescribed, modes and contents of learning.

This need to see the educational process from the child's point of view begins before the child goes to school. For example, Steven was three when he was faced at home by material from a Hearing and Speech Centre. He had been identified as in need of speech therapy. So he was offered by a speech therapist a succession of images, arranged in strips, like stills in a film or filmstrip, depicting, alternately, a crocodile, a mouse, a crocodile, a mouse...and so on.

At the top of the page, in Marion Richardson script, it says: 'ah-ee/a-i'. We adults understand, after puzzled scrutiny that 'ah' is the noise the crocodile is supposed to make, and that 'ee' is what mice do. Steven, we assume, is being trained in two of his long vowel sounds. On another page, 'oo' is represented by a drawing of the west wind with a mouth blowing. 'ai' is an eye. 'b' is a ball, 't' is a tap and 'm' a motorcycle. Later, 'b' is a ball again, and 'oy' is a parrot. Put the two together and you get, of course, 'boy'.

Then the rules change. A girl holding a teddy stands for 'my', a bearded man in dungarees is 'Mike'. A page in front of me now looks like this: a white woman is 'Kay'. A black woman is 'Kate'. A diagrammatic cake is 'cake'. We also have a 'cage' and a 'case' with relevant, if banal, drawings.

Of course, the writers of this material would tell us that it is linked with what the speech therapist says. They would also argue that they are not interested in the meaning of words, that the cards are there only to prompt the sounds. I would argue that Steven and all other children can produce images of far greater vigour and interest than the images presented here. These drawings have been made with one kind of line, the sort of line that is concerned with what is called photographic representation (though photographs are infinitely more subtle). They are stereo-typical: crocodiles snarl (ah) and mice are meek ('eek'). I have been unable to gain permission to reprint them, but I can include a drawing by Steven that contrasts, in its vigour, with what he was subjected to in his therapy sessions.

The child subjected to this material will be confused. Speech therapists, educational psychologists and other visitors to schools seem unable to understand that many things impinge on a child's consciousness. See it from a child's point of view: those children throw a *real* ball around on the playground; there is a school lunch I can still taste on my tongue, there is a painting I have just left, because I've been brought to this room, 'My friend Mark has a new baby sister', 'My friend Joanna's mother has died of cancer...' But she must look at this strange piece of paper in front of her and try to see what it is for, and she must forget the games, the food, the art, the birth, the death, and concentrate on croco-diles (ah) and mice (eek).

Two children have speech problems. One lives in Ipswich, one in Yorkshire. They are each presented with images of a mine (a wheel on a scaffold on a slag heap). Are we to ask them to see this image in the same way? I teach in both Yorkshire and Suffolk. Are both groups of children to be expected to sound vowels in the same way? Are both of these two children, given their experi-ences, to be expected to respond to these images identically? Or do speech therapists produce different material for different parts of the country?

I should say at this point that the company responsible for this material was asked for permission to reprint the material described above. They asked for a sight of my comments on it, and were sent an early draft of the above. They did not reply. Hence my wooden descriptions of their material.

There are various ways of getting, momentarily, inside children's view of school.

1. Adults' recollections of school

The first is to try to remember words that rise from the silted memories of our own early schooldays, and to share these words in groups; and then to reflect in our own schools on the memories those words stand for:

[written; headteacher]

I remember the deep scratches in the lid of the desk, a lid that you lifted up, unlike any other table I had ever seen...I remember some-one saying we should all draw a margin before we started to write, and I didn't know what a margin was...

[spoken; ex-headteacher]

I can't remember the very early days...I went to junior school, no, first I went to this infant school, the first day in the junior school, it was on the other side of the playground, it was all kind of dusty, somehow, a dusty memory, it must have been a dusty day, little dots in the eye, misty...The bell went, we all had to line up, I didn't know where to line up because I'd never been there before, and I found my big brother, I got near him, you're probably safe with your big brother... when the bell went and I got into the right place, Jack Hobbs, Mr Hobbs, I suppose he was called Jack Hobbs because of the cricketer, called out some names, my name was in this list and my brother's name was in this list, and we got the cane because we'd been scrump-ing in the vicarage...that's my earliest memory...

And walking down this corridor in the primary school and looking into cupboards at bottles with strange things in them...

And I was well pleased because Alf Burden was pleased with my handwriting...

Another memory. We were football-mad, this was the late forties and I hadn't any football boots and one day Alf Burden turned up with a sack of football boots with cogs nailed in and he says try them on...They'd been there for years they were all disintegrating...

[spoken; housewife]

I can remember the teacher holding a flash card about 6" x 5" with letters on them. I can remember painting at an easel and being told off because I flicked paint on to a boy called Melvyn and I told him it was rain & the teacher told me off...We had a new teacher and before we were allowed to take pictures home, and I'd folded this drawing up and put it in my pocket, and this new teacher said, where is it? and she smacked me...

When I was 7 I was at this private school, the head was an alcoholic and people were leaving quickly and then I was moved...well, the head was a man, a nice man with a drink problem, and he put these sums on the board and they were fractions and there was a 1 over a 4 and I didn't know what that meant and he put them on the board and I was sitting next to this girl & I whispered to her what does that mean?

[written; nurse]

A load of us were being farmed out to another school because our school was being rebuilt after a tree fell on it. I was on the board for being able to do laces up and kept one of the boys in all through his morning break because I insisted on doing his shoes up but I couldn't. You were only allowed to wear pull-on plimsolls if you couldn't tie a bow.

I remember making a model of a church with a wedding party made of toilet rolls, and cutting pictures of couples out of *The Suffolk Free Press*. I remember learning songs that my parents didn't know, and that seemed strange.

I did a picture of me with my mum and one teacher said to another, Maybe I shouldn't take it home for fear of upsetting my mum. I'd done her sort of square with no neck. I remember that as the most difficult thing – when you had to pretend you couldn't hear teachers and when to acknowledge what they said.

What emerges from these recollections is, firstly, that most of the significant things that happen in a school (as far as children are allowed to see) are merely administrative data. You are only allowed to wear pull-on plimsolls if you can't tie a bow. There are margins, for example – in every sense of the word. We must draw them, and probably we must put the date at the top of the page before we start to write. In Mrs A's class, we must put our names on the back of the drawing; in Mr B's, we put them on the front. Most of these rules change every September, and learning the new ones comes before any education. ('I think I've just about got them into shape,' someone always says around the beginning of October). One school insists that the children, however fluent their writing, keep it short, as otherwise too much time will be used up later on copying the material out for display.

And there are confusions betrayed by a fact that the teacher consistently ignored: the children had never been there before. How much less threatening we could make school by acting on our awareness that children have been suddenly imprisoned in institutions utterly different from any that they have ever known before; we might try to imagine, or remember, the strength of the bond between parent and child that all the adults in the setting, with varying degrees of commitment, are colluding in breaking.

Secondly, children are far more aware of crucial elements of life that adults consider secret: 'The head was an alcoholic'; 'I remember that as the most difficult thing – when you had to pretend you couldn't hear teachers and when to acknowledge what they said'. These examples are like photographs in an album, making us aware in an over-focussed way of what we might, except for these snapshots, have forgotten. But there are in these reminiscences hints of what it is like to be a child in a classroom.

Children remember the violence, the negative, the horror: 'we got the cane – on my first day of school!' laughs one headteacher. Another classroom ancillary worker said to me about her schooldays, 'I had to go – so I went'. Children are also aware of inconsistencies between teachers, and in one teacher's behaviour.

The nurse quoted above also had some comments about my theme of hiding:

> ...it's universal. Some time...I will take you to St Andrew's [local mental hospital; name changed]. I can't believe you will see anywhere an example of more blatant concealment. In the reception area there is pink carpet, a chandelier, and a staircase that looks as though it might feature in your Austen scenario (see Introduction) but directly around the corner this makes way for lino and strip lights; concrete staircases and Ken Kesey [author of *One Flew over the Cuckoo's Nest*]... the illusion it creates is self-defeating...

2. The questionnaire

A way of finding out about the view today's children have of their schools is to give them a questionnaire. But the questions will be ours, and children, too accustomed to our questions, have developed strategies for keeping their insights to themselves. This is especially so should those insights conflict with our ways of looking at the world. Children are so used to answering us in adult-pleasing ways, it is difficult to get through to less adult-infected points of view. In an attempt to do this, I asked 11-year-old children at St. Mary's RCVP School, Ipswich, to write questions that might provoke answers that might, in turn, expose to adults what children 'really' think of school. Of course, this exercise was only marginally successful, because it came as a surprise to the children. In my 1993 book in this series, I noted that a boy asked to comment on videos of his performance in dance lessons was struck almost dumb: 'I don't really know what to say about it...I get my curves in...I don't know...'

Becoming informed about children's views of their schools will only be possible when such an attempt is part of everyday school life, and not a one-off for a research project or a book. Anyway, these were the questions that, in groups of five, the children at St.

Mary's wrote. I provoked the adding of the occasional 'Why?'

- What is your favourite place in school, and why?
- What do you think of the classrooms, and why?
- What is your favourite thing in the classroom? Why?
- What improvements could be made to school?
- What's your favourite lesson? And why? Plus: what's your favourite part in it? And why?
- What's your worst part in it? Why?
- If you had a chance of coming to school or not would you come?
- If you would not go to school if you had the choice of going to school or not what would you do about your education?
- Do you agree with what your teacher says and does? Why?
- What things about dinner ladies do you like?
- What things about dinner ladies don't you like?
- Are you scared of the dinner ladies?
- Do you feel safe around them?

A teacher interviewed five five-year-olds (four of them Bangladeshi) with this questionnaire, and pictures of certain worries emerged immediately. 'I don't like the classroom,' said one. 'It's too noisy'. There was general agreement that assembly was too noisy as well. Dinner ladies were alright, largely – 'sometimes they play with you' – but 'one makes you eat brown bread and sweetcorn'. Noise was a central concern for these children, and, of course, this was connected to the fact that the loud speech was in a language that was their second one, and they could not always understand it.

Some year six children also mentioned the need for quiet. They preferred the library 'because I like reading', 'because I like poems and books', 'because I can gather my thoughts and feelings in silence'. Kate liked the 'bookshelf' in her room 'stacked with ideas and memories'. But the most telling responses here were of two boys, one of whom preferred 'the stairs near the class 3S, because there is always nobody there' and another who liked the 'deputy heads office because its high up'.

It was sad, given that these children were about to leave the security of a classroom of their own for the corridor-travelling of a secondary school, that many of them liked best in the whole school 'my classroom because it feels like home because I have been there so long'; 'my classroom, because I have been here for three years running'. 'My favitove thing,' writes another girl 'is Jaclyn, because she is nice to sit next to'. A boy comments: 'my favrout thing is my tray because if it wasn't there I would be lost

72

where would I put my things'.

The message here is about security, and that need not make us into primary, chauvinist child-protectors, intent on home corners and class bases, and desperate to berate our secondary colleagues with all sorts of sins concerned with lack of child-centredness. After all, life involves movement and travel. But we can learn from these answers that children are often interested in finding more opportunities than are commonly available for quiet reflection, 'gathering my thoughts and feelings in silence'. Delwyn and Eva Tattum (in *Social Educational and Personal Development*, 1992) quote children in their first year at secondary school who confirm that peace, or the lack of it, is a serious worry: 'Getting on the bus worries me because everyone starts to push you...I was surprised [at the dinners] the queue was terrible...'

We stereotype children in dozens of ways: as constant skippers, chasers, kickers, throwers, as on an Opie book cover (though there is no hint of stereotype inside these marvellous books); or as innocents abroad; or as television watchers, utterly unable to entertain themselves; or (somewhat fundamentally) as conceived in iniquity and born in sin. The quiet thinker is less well known, but these children show us that the reflective girl or boy can be found at the 'stairs near the class 3S, because there is always nobody there'.

Emma was typical of eight of the twelve children answering the questionnaire when she wrote, 'I wish we could have a capit for the floor'. This was in a high-ceilinged room with a wooden floor, where every scrape of a chair's legs drowned whoever was speaking. It seems that quiet was important to these children, much as it was to the five-year-olds quoted earlier.

The question of midday supervisory assistants shows us that elements in school life that are seen, usually, as the least important by senior management teams are often of vital importance to children. While to the teachers the lunch hour is a failed attempt at a break (these days mostly polluted with meeting after meeting after meeting), to the child it is the continuation of real life. There is a common feeling that 'dinner ladies' should listen to all sides of the story before making decisions. 'I do not like it when someone is being nasty and all they say is "Stay Away"'; 'I don't like some of them because they don't let you explane things they go right ahed and tell you off'; 'Sometimes they shout at you without getting all the facts'. This is a point worth widening: from the adult's point of view, the priority is often the restoration of order and quiet. The minor injustice of a wrongly aimed telling-off is of little consequence. But children have a strong sense of fairness, and they want full inquiries. 'Sometimes,' complains Jacob, 'they tell you off for something you dident do'. Some children, of course, merely jump the steps.

The children at another school show us that they need what staff at Cavell First School call (chapter 1) 'talk-it-out policies', and (even more important) ways of finding time to make those policies real. To *realise* them.

In September 1991, I spoke to five dinner ladies about their perspectives on the children for an article for the *Times Educational Supplement* ('Stories to dine out on', September 1992). Some of them left me shrugging miserably. It may not be pleasant to read comments like the following, but it is important to recognise that such perspectives are widely held, and that teachers all too rarely come up against them. If they wanted to be better informed, they might leave that table in the corner of the pub, where they habitually gather for a Friday lunchtime, or for the celebration of a colleague's promotion, and join the drinkers at the bar, who might well agree with these dinner ladies:

> Standards have gone down, no doubt about it. There isn't so much discipline, is there? There's no manners. They push, they shove...

> It's the home as well, the kids on this estate can't use a knife and fork properly when they come here, they can't sit at a table...You should see them in the dining hall. They come shooshing by, you have to shout at them, 'Oi! stop', or they'll knock you over...

> They don't respect adults. It's not the teachers' fault. One of my dinner ladies [this is the school cook speaking] goes about with her overall undone, sometimes she walks across the dining hall without her shoes on, how can you respect someone like that? The children call her by her first name. They don't say please and thank you at the hatch.

Hannah cut through all the semi-officialdom of the questionnaire exercise when she wrote, in answer to the question about dinner ladies and safety: 'Sometimes, well I do with my mum Mrs Miller because she's a dinner lady and I love her'. And Emma made me shake my head in nervous gratitude on the part of all adults in respect of children: 'I feel safe with anyone I know'. I wanted to respond with the words of Charles Causley's poem 'School at four o'clock':

Listen. Through the clear shell of air the voices
Still strike like water from the mountain bed;
The cry of these who to a certain valley
Hungry and innocent came. And were not fed.

Effective INSET might well be based on informing ourselves as teachers of the worries and obsessions the children in our school have, and in then working, with the children, to the betterment of the environment. Tattum and Tattum also print, in a table, summaries of research which show that bullying is a common worry for all transferees; that administrative factors, like losing things, are in the front of these pupils' minds; that the size of the new school is a worry. How much more eloquent, though, are the written comments of the children themselves. If this concern with bullying is there at secondary transfer stage, we might as well be fairly certain that it is there too at the infant/junior transfer, and indeed at the point where the children first leave home to go to the nursery or the playgroup or the reception class.

3. Listening to children

This is the most obvious way of finding out about children's perceptions of school, but adults rarely do this. Writers like Douglas Barnes and James Britton wrote thirty years ago about how the experts in talk, the teachers, give themselves most of the practice, leaving the children, still relatively inexperienced talkers, little spaces between the powerful institutional words. The Opies have time and time again (*The Lore and Language of Schoolchildren*,1959, and *The Singing Game*, 1985) demonstrated how listening to children on the playground (and elsewhere) informs us of their feelings, joys and fears, and of what we might call, using the word in the neutral sense, their culture. They found variations on the following rhyme all over England, Wales and Scotland:

Mr MacDonald is a good man,
  He goes to church on Sunday.
He prays to God to give him strength
  To whip the kids on Monday...

Other writers and anthologists, like Frank Shaw (*You know me Anty Nelly*, Wolfe, 1970), who worked on Merseyside in the sixties, offer us glimpses – here into the child rushing to school:

And I keep singing in my heart,
Don't mark me late,
Don't mark me late.

and here into children waiting for their names on the register:

What's yer name?
　Mary Jane.
Where d'you live?
　Down the grid.
What number?
　Cucumber.
What house?
　Pig Scouse.

Having an ear for these rhymes stops us making up patently false titles about 'an early start to poetry'. Poetry (Frank Shaw quotes the German folklorist Herder as saying) 'is heard on the lips of the common people'. Listening also helps us to glimpse how children see teachers, and what their fears are about school. Sometimes what we discover is no more or less than a relish for language itself, almost regardless of its meanings. A girl in Slough had friends who told me she could rhyme any name. 'James,' I said:

James
Bom Bames
Lick a Lames
Five Fames
Five Fames
Bom Bames
(That's how you rhyme James)

I worked for three days in a school in Sunderland, and, on the playground one lunchtime, called three girls 'Geordies'. 'We're not Geordies,' one of them said scornfully. 'We're Mackems'. 'And what am I?' I asked. 'You're a Poshy,' the girls replied. An example of other rhymes that tell us something, if we will listen, about children's view of school is:

Please Miss, me mother Miss
I've got to tell you this Miss
That I, Miss, won't Miss,
Be in school tomorrow, Miss

But there has been a disturbing new tendency in the last few years. As Marian Whitehead tells us ('Born again phonics and the nursery rhyme revival', *English in Education*, Autumn 1993), new research in the teaching of reading has linked 'learning your sounds' with 'young children's learning of nursery rhymes'. This research is, as Whitehead says, 'exciting in its foregrounding of the poetic and playful aspects of language structures and function'. But (to quote Whitehead again) 'much of the phonological awareness research is...dismissive of the chanting of nursery rhymes for the purposes of social bonding and group participation'.

I would go further. What else will those who are concerned with the control of children hi-jack? Nursery rhymes, often subversive and anarchic, are concerned with the chipping away of adult monoliths. 'Children,' as Whitehead puts it, 'are about subverting the power structure they cannot avoid'. And here we have proponents of a controlling training system (phonic reading methods) taking from children that very means of subversion.

4. *Reading what children write*

I have given examples of this elsewhere in the book and in others (*The Expressive Arts*, 1993, and *Here Comes the Assembly Man*, 1989). We need to read children's writing more carefully. This means all their writing – but there are some ways of getting work that may be especially illuminating. I asked children in Basildon to close their eyes. Then I said:

> I'm going to take you back thousands of years, to the very first morning in the history of the world. There's nothing in the world at all, except you and a grey mist. You are walking through a clean, pure grey mist. It's utterly unpolluted, because the world is brand new, only half an hour old. As you walk through this new place, three colours shine out of the mist. What are they? Write them down.
>
> Now write a word for each of those colours that tells us more about it. What sort of blue, or green, or purple is it?
>
> Now, just as you are getting used to the mist and its three colours, three sounds come out of the mist. What are they? What's making them?
>
> In this clean place, there are suddenly three smells. What are they?
>
> You come across two objects in the mist, one a surprise, one to be expected. What are they?
>
> A signpost is pointing to something a long way off on the horizon. What is it?

I walk through the dark grey mist
trying to find the path to a new world
When something caught my attention.
It was the three most beautiful colours
in the world,
the first one was a golden sparkling yellow
the second one was gleaming red
like a burning fire flickering in a warm
cosy house
and the third colour of all was
dark blue from the sea smashing into
Waves on the way to somewhere
far away from here.
I started to walk towards the three colours
When I heard something
the first thing I heard was people reading
poems
there were some funny some sad some
some good some bad then
I heard people dancing, singing songs
and drinking wine

people were laughing and clapping
and then it disappeared
after a while a third sound came
it was waves crashing into each other
on a windy day When the sounds had died
down I saw something that I'd seen before
and meant nothing to me at all
but I looked around and I saw a big
shining block of gold waiting to be picked
up and taken home.
While I was staring at the gold a warm
friendly hand tapped me on the sholder
I turned around and there stood a man with
silk clothes on it was God.
He said "from now on you will be
one of them"
His finger turned and pointed to the horizon
There I saw three angels sitting on soft
White fluffy clouds
each drifting away into the sky.
Each angel was wearing different silks
the first angel was wearing a golden yellow
silk the second one was wearing a dark

by
Katie
Vernum

red silk like a burning fire
the last one was wearing a dark blue
silk like the sea and the

5. Conceptual maps

Draw a map of school, showing what the most important parts are. John Cotton is now in his late sixties, and this was how he remembered his primary school. He has drawn like an adult about the child he was, and how he felt to be there in that school. This potential is open to all of us, and might make us more aware of what it is like to be a child in a school.

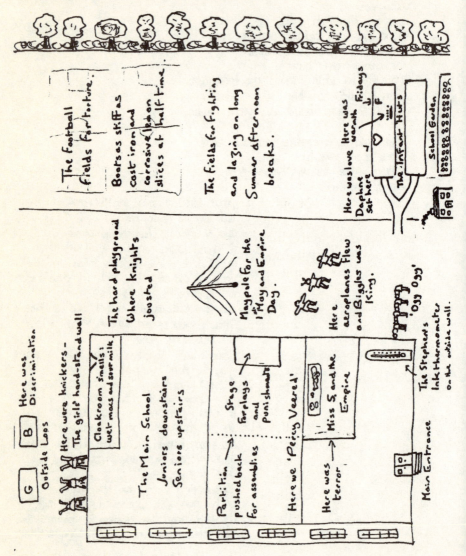

Headstone Lane All Age School 1930

CHAPTER FOUR

Evil in return: Violence in schools

It can't be helped;
It must be done.
So down with your breeches
And out with your bum.

      quoted in James Joyce, *A Portrait of the Artist as a Young Man*

This chapter will not only discuss bullying as usually understood – 'an interaction,' as someone ponderously put it, 'in which a more dominant individual or group intentionally causes distress to a less dominant individual or group' – but also the notion of conflict: between pupils, and between teachers; between pupils and teachers; and between teachers and the authorities under whom they work: local education authorities, advisers, inspectors, governors and, increasingly over the past few years, central government.

It may not always seem obvious to local authority advisers and officers that the managers of a school that searches for autonomy for pupils cannot logically deprive teachers of autonomy. But it is obvious to most teachers, as planning of the curriculum and indeed most of the policy-making parts of the school agenda are taken away from them, and as they are vilified in the press and by politicians. It is clear to teachers that an authority or government that prescribes what they may or may not teach, and how this teaching may or may not be done, cannot expect them to offer children a stronger purchase on their learning. It is like cooking a vegetarian meal with an entirely carnivorous cookbook. If teachers are dictated to, so, by extension, are children.

And we might say two things about that dictation. First, it is an inappropriate and indeed dangerous training for citizens living in what is still called a democratic society. And second, it is closely related to the issue of bullying.

A. S. Neill says in *Summerhill* (1968) that it is not possible to approve of children if you do not approve of yourself. This seems to me to be analagous to another statement: however much you bravely attempt to sing 'in [your] chains like the sea' (as Dylan Thomas puts it), you cannot offer freedom while you are in those chains.

I have noted before how the violence of some kinds of managerial thinking is exposed. Headteachers on a course about appointing staff commented after a role-play interview (*Here Comes the Assembly Man*, 1989): 'You didn't really tear the candidate apart... You've got to really hammer the candidate...When I get a deputy I expect to burn him (*sic*) out and send him on to a headship...' Violence is endemic in schools, and it does not emerge initially from pupils. The language used by many adults is violent in its imprisoning tone and diction. Example: Midday Supervisory Assistant: 'Can I have something unpleasant for Jessica to do?' Teacher: 'Give her her reading book. She can copy out a few pages of that' (Essex, November 1993). Setting aside for another time, another book, what this incident is teaching the child about the place of reading in her life, I nevertheless note now the violence, the imposition of a powerful person on a weaker one.

Again, the atmosphere in many schools is claustrophobic in its grassless, concrete setting. One school in the north of England that I know well is surrounded on the one side by a railway yard, and on the others by noisy, dangerous roads. The violence and the potential for violence of both these settings is evident day by day to the children in, for example, the accidents and the dehumanising labour going on around them, and in the broken glass stuck along one of the walls.

And pupils, as a rule, have their personal space invaded by peremptory commands: 'Take this tray to the hatch...Stop that now'. As teachers, therefore, we have to address the problems of our own violence, whether it is physical or emotional, in order to understand pupils' violence. We also have to accept what we usually cannot control: the violence of the setting in which their schools are placed. This means accepting that politics, like the air we breathe and the water we drink, is a literally vital element in all our lives, in private or in social modes, and that our well-being depends on a vigilance against pollution just as much in the politics as it does in the air and the water.

Indeed, violence is endemic to society, and we must place bullying in school in the context of society's attitudes to strength and weakness. This consideration is not limited to what is usually seen as crime, but is also concerned with economic power and weakness, and the way in which the glorifying of economic power can lead to bullying of one kind or another. Arguably, male bullying on the playground is merely what Beatrix Campbell called on *Woman's Hour* (17 June 1993) 'the continuation of what men have always done exacerbated by poverty'. Certainly it is not as easy as the politicians and the media sometimes seem to think to detach official violence – war and policing for example – from the violence that causes easy disapproval in school, bullying and (I write in the wake of the James Bulger trial) murder.

Nor is it as easy as many suggest to detach male violence in war from violence in the streets. GOTCHA was a headline about the sinking of an enemy battleship on its flight from battle. But it would serve for any bully in any situation anywhere. If we glorify individualistic, economic power, we should not be surprised when that power is used in non-economic ways; when that power is used in the street to express physical or assumed racial superiority. If, through television and advertising, we glorify possessions, we should not be surprised when the poorest in our society, taunted as they are with these images of plenty, react in anger at their deprivation and become violent.

Then again, teachers violate each other. One experienced teacher – I will call him Michael – found the quiet probationer, 'Sarah', an irritant. From her point of view, she was an inexperienced professional, just out of college, and as a naturally shy person she kept quiet in the staffroom. From Michael's point of view, though, she needed to be 'brought out'. So when he placed the whoopee cushion in her usual chair, and when she sat on it and then ran from the room crying, all he could say was, 'I just wanted to know if she'd react to anything'.

Some reference is necessary to the violence that pupils can inflict on teachers, though you would not think so from reading the current literature on the subject. The broadcaster Danny Baker told this story during his Radio 5 programme *Morning Edition* some time in 1993. As I was on the M25 at the time, my memories are all recalled from some time later and may not be a perfect record. A middle-aged Welsh teacher at Baker's single-sex South London secondary school was memorably and coolly depicted by Baker as an inept old fool: shambling, smiling, eager to please everybody, he was given an especially bad time by the boys, who had no respect for him. One day, in a pathetic attempt to curry favour with a rough class (that is how the young Baker saw it; teachers, no doubt, will see it differently; parents will see it in many different ways) he brought into school his elderly mother's crystal wireless set. We can easily and sadly imagine his lesson: 'You boys have your stereo, your hi-fi, your pop music...when my mother was a child, when they wanted to listen to the radio, this is what they used...She has kept this set all her life...'

The teacher was called away, Baker reports. And when he returned to the classroom he found the crystal set smashed on the top of his desk. 'He stared at it for a minute, and a boy said, "He's crying, he's crying..." and the teacher walked out of the room'.

We note here Baker's objective tone. He is still as interested as he was when he was the boy who first noticed the teacher crying. His tone of voice was clinical. He spoke with an almost Hemingwayesque detachment, a cold exploration of that boy-master relationship. I feel glimmerings of the same clinical interest, too, though I am ashamed on behalf of all girls and boys who have tortured a teacher: Mr Chips as car crash on the motorway.

Another Radio 4 story: having been brought up in Africa, a new girl at an English public school has never seen the local countryside. The other girls blindfold her and call her through a patch of nettles.

Viciousness and sentimentality often travel together: the latter is what Philip Larkin characterised as 'the costly aversion of the eyes from death', and the critic Leavis called 'emotion in excess of the facts'. Pre-adolescents who hug soft toys and small animals will, minutes later, torment each other into storms of tears. We can see this dizzying mix in the triumphant shouting of fundamentalist religion of various brands. It's evident in the extreme loyalists in Northern Ireland, where the Roman Catholic Church and all her followers are abused. We can see it in the fundamentalism of Islam, where there is new talk about *The Protocols of the Elders of Zion*, and the anti-Semitism we thought we'd seen the last of years ago.

I saw this morning an example of the conjunction of viciousness and sentimentality. A tabloid newspaper printed on the front page two images: a model dressed in male-fantasy underwear, and a banner headline about the recent sexual assault and murder of a young woman. The viciousness is obvious, and the sentimentality is in the falsified woman, of course, the decadent view of notions surrounding the word 'love'; but it's also in the media's refusal to see, in the commercial interests of proprietors, that there is a link between pornography and sexual violence.

A vicious sentimentality is present whenever human experience is subjected to falsifying structures – in, for example, simplistic assessment in education, or in the rule of the love of money over the love of our human natures. The violence of children on the playground, then, has to be placed into the context I have tried to sketch above.

More conventional bullying is graphically described by a boy in Cedric Cullingford's 1994 article 'The Attitudes of Children to their Environment' (*Cambridge Journal of Education*, 24.1):

Some people don't like me probably because, like, if they start kicking me and that I just get 'old of them and throw them across the playground or something because I get annoyed...I try and run away but they just get me and try and like beat me up and that. They throw me in the air. They like lift me up and then wing me like that. It's really horrible.

It is interesting to note here that the boy tried to do what adults always say he should do: walk away from it. By contrast, Annabelle Dixon teaches her children words that help them find another more creative solution (see chapter 1). Joan Webster, also in chapter 1, teaches children ways of 'talking it out'.

I watched Jo Palmer teaching a drama lesson about bullying at All Saints School, Lawshall, in Suffolk, and I type up the following from my notes. The children are seven and eight. The school is in a rural part of Suffolk. The outsider coming here for the first time would not expect there to be much violence around or in this school, and she would probably be right.

It is a cold bright early December morning. The children gather round Jo on the floor of the hall. It's a pleasant modern extension to an old building, and outside the hall, just down the corridor, I can see the original exterior of the building, now part of an inner wall, where children at the school when the extension was finished have dug their names on the old bricks. Outside the windows, the flat, calm West Suffolk fields spread as far as I can see. There's a church which, I discover later, is locked except on Sundays, despite the apparent peace of the area. I walk round the outside of the group, comprising young teacher and children, with my notebook and pen. 'Can we remember,' asks Jo, 'the rules about drama?' A child says something I can't hear. 'Good girl,' says Jo. 'If something upsets you, you just stop. And the other rules are Cut. Action. And Freeze...'

There's a lot more question and answer as Jo and the children sit in their circle in the middle of the hall floor. She asks them, 'What is bullying?' and they reply:

Being horrible to other people...taking away a book they're in the middle of ...calling people names...punching...tripping people up...taking friends away from people...

Jo encourages a quiet child to speak. 'I think the same...hurting people,' he says, not wanting to say anything, really, and therefore taking the line of least resistance. Then Jo asks a question that can have only one right answer, and the children have a fifty-fifty chance of getting it right, and getting it right will tell Jo nothing about their learning, will give nothing in the way of material to assess. All education is, technically at least, about questions. There are so many kinds: real ones, like the ones they hear at home, before they start school: 'Do you want more potatoes?' Then there are questions that are really commands, that they have to learn to read differently from the way they read those home questions: 'Would you like to sit here, now, Martha?'

Then there are those questions that follow convention by finishing with question marks, but which are really spot-checks: 'What are the boats the Vikings came in?...they are...' There are very few questions to which the teacher doesn't know the answer, and yet these are often the most productive, the most educational questions: 'What do you mean by that?...' 'Can you explain that a bit more?...' We rarely ask these questions, I suspect, because they lead to long silences, to embarrassment (who is going to fill this terrible space?), or even to distress: this child doesn't know, but the silence, the embarrassment, the distress might well be the channel for her learning.

The questions we do ask are often control questions, the imposition of our wills on theirs: 'Would you like to stop that now, Ben

– immediately' (long significant look. Ben sheepishly returns from sandtray to exercise book. Teacher returns to hearing another child read, her professionalism proved yet again).

Jo's question here is: 'If it happens only once, is it bullying?' She means them to understand that it's only bullying if it 'happens again and again', but the children stand up against this interpretation: 'Wayne [the victim in an anecdote Jo had used to illustrate her theory] might think it was bullying even it only happened once'. Another question Jo asks suggests that she wants the children to understand it is only bullying if it is deliberate, but, again, one of the children resists this: 'Wayne might think it was bullying even if the bully didn't mean it...'

The children warm up, walking round the room, obeying Jo's instruction to make no sound with their feet, then getting faster, still walking, and eventually running, quietly. 'FREEZE!' shouts Jo, and they do. Then she shouts 'FAST FORWARD' and they scamper round the room, like water going down a plughole. 'BACKWARDS!...FREEZE!...' Recent research has suggested that children in school rarely get their heartbeat up to the levels required to provide a sort of fragile bastion against eventual heart disease, and this sort of warm-up activity is valuable, if relatively low level, health education.

'I want to teach you,' Jo says as they calm down in the centre of the room,

> What it feels like to be a bully...I'm going to tell you about a girl called Alice...she had been bullied by a boy called Daniel. Daniel has been taking money. But he's been blaming her. In front of all her friends he's been saying she's taken the money. He's going to be very unpleasant to Alice...

She looks around at the children, making eye contact with each one. This is at least in part a health warning that some of the lesson may distress them, and I recall the one-word escape clause she has given them: FREEZE.

Then she divides the class up into two mixed-sex groups, Daniels (bullies) and Alices (victims), and she puts the Alices in a tight little circle in the middle of the room, facing out. 'Remember, you can put your hand up to stop whenever you like'. The Daniels are standing and looking down on the Alices. Jo tells them to say bullying things to the Alice group, 'but you mustn't touch them'. One boy asks if they can use swearwords, but Jo doesn't hear him. I would have been interested in the answer. Then the Daniels slowly circle: 'Shorty...naughty...you are [inaudible]...Nobody likes you...you smell...' As this goes on, Jo swaps Alices for Daniels. The new Alices, formerly Daniels, sit foetus-like, looking genuinely miserable, not looking up, resembling homeless beggars in a shop doorway. Afterwards Jo asks them: 'Were you miserable?' 'No'. Jo says to the Daniels, 'You aren't trying hard enough...This time we are going to think first about what we are going to do'.

Thinking is something difficult to assess, of course, because it isn't behaviourally observable. So we underrate it. It is preferable to many teachers to see the hand shoot up with that sudden audible, even vocalised intake of breath, than to feel a silence that might contain thinking, but which, again, might not. Here Jo is doing something relatively unusual: insisting on peace while the children contemplate, reflect on what they might do and say next.

The Alices close their eyes and the Daniels encircle them, moving round, whispering at first, then getting louder and louder, and it is, at least as far as I am concerned, a genuinely disturbing crescendo: 'I'm going to kill you. You smell. I hate you. You're gonna get told off. You took the money. Where is it? Where is it? Where is it? Hate. Kill. Hate. Kill...' This is very different from the earlier attempt. Even bullying requires thought and planning. And then, just as I am being reminded of that terrible scene in Golding's *The Lord of the Flies* where the boys chant 'Kill the pig!... Kill the pig!', Jo shouts 'Cut!' This time the Alices admit that they felt 'scared...upset...terrified...' The bullies felt 'fine...I was scared they'd tell on me...I felt I was succeeding in chasing them off...I felt guilty when I could see they were getting sad...sad...'

Melanie, who has a lot to say, and who sometimes skips around on the edge of things without apparently taking a great deal of notice, says suddenly: 'People bully because they're being bullied', and I am suddenly reminded of Auden's lucid, honest lines (note especially the word 'learn': children do not 'naturally' 'know' this fact): 'I and the public know/What all schoolchildren learn,/Those to whom evil is done/Do evil in return.' ('September 1939'), and then I think of the unthinkable violence of the James Bulger murder. And surely, amid all the talk of innate evil, here is more evidence of a truth I've already hinted at: that individuals suppressed economically, yet surrounded by evidence of others' material possessions – on television, in advertising – will perhaps incline towards revengeful evil.

Jo asks them, 'What can we change? We can't change what the bully can do, but if we are victims there are things we can do...' She puts them into groups of three. One is to act a bully, one a victim, and the third person is there to evaluate what the victim does – which is to insist, quietly, 'No'. One evaluator intervenes, unable to resist the dramatic pressure of seeing an acting bully jabbing her face into her much smaller victim's. She pushes them apart, like a boxing referee, until the bully says, 'That's what we're supposed to be doing!' 'Oh yeah!' Other groups manage well, the bully leaning scarily forward, the victim simply saying, 'No'.

Then Jo tells them about 'fogging'. This is pretending you're not upset when you're being bullied. Jo tells the victims to say, 'You might think so,' in an unconcerned voice when they're being called names. Jo shouts, 'Action!' Melanie skips happily about as her friends carry on working. One tiny fair-haired boy says plaintively to Jo, 'I'm not very good at bullying'. She puts her arm on his shoulders and gives him a little hug.

Both of these activities are echoed the next day when I hear a feature about drunken driving on Radio 4's *Today* programme. Convicted motorists gain a reduction in their sentences if they go on a course designed to demonstrate the results of their behaviour. At one point, we hear a tutor on the course acting the part of a persuasive friend in a pub: 'Go on, have just one, it won't make any difference...' and the driver is repeating, 'No thank you, I'm not drinking this evening, I'll just have a coke'. This is training in proper, socialised behaviour. And it resembles what Jo is teaching the children. The difference between the two settings is that the adults have been faced with the consequences of their actions; they have been educated in other parts of the course and in real life in the physiological and psychological effects of alcohol. What is the equivalent education for the children in Jo's class? In helping them to protect themselves against bullies, is she also educating them?

The last technique Jo shows the children is called 'Broken Record'. This is where you repeat the same sentence whatever the provocation. Jo leans into little Rachel and demands she has a go on Rachel's bike. 'I don't lend my bike,' says Rachel, time and time again. 'I don't lend my bike'. Jo praises her for her resistance, and then shouts 'Cut!' Later the children drew some pictures and wrote about bullying:

Theres a little boy here. He looks good to Bully Youre a stupid little worm!
Give me your sweets. I thought oh good. My brain said stop! but I did'nt

I was frightened. I tried to run through and They kicked out at me. I tried to
think but my brain couldn't think. My heart was pounding. People were
calling me names like "pigface" and "shrimp" and "little baby" and "baby
worm" and things like that. I tried to keep calm but it didn't work.

Thomas

Horrible demolished legs
Rude yucky swearwords
Frightening like you are watching a
scary film
Really loud like my brain is
going wrong

I feel awsome and strong
She is a wimp and small
It is great to kick people

Lewis

I didn't think I could do it
Then I look at her in the middle
my friends gathered around her
I was in charge
now I can do what I want

Jenny

These pieces capture, through the catalyst of the drama, much of
the essence of the bully/victim situation. 'My brain said stop! but
I did'nt. I tried to think but my brain couldn't think. I tried to
keep calm but it didn't work. Horrible demolished legs. It is great
to kick people. My friends gathered around her. I was in charge
now. I can do what I want'. I note in the last two sentences an
echo of Ted Hughes's poem 'The Hawk': 'My eye has permitted
no change./I am going to keep things like this.' If occasionally
this work resembles training rather than education, it also enables
children to face up to what bullying is, in a realistic and yet safe
context.

The most prominent form of attack on children at the moment is
sexual and physical abuse. Talking to teachers, I found deep cyni-
cism about their relationship with social workers and the police
when it came to dealing with this issue.

I worked with a family therapy unit with children who had been
abused, and I did my long essay on it...I've dealt with adult survivors

...My mother's a clinical psychologist and I went to work with her for a year and my she is a behaviourist and it just inspired me that you should teach children ways of behaving and ways of responding to things that would equip them so that they could actually cope better and instead of all the drama and all the melodrama that tends to surround the subject...it was a practical way of going on...I believe if you change people's behaviour you also change their attitudes... '

I listened with concern to this, because it ran counter to my conviction that as educators we are concerned, above all else you might say, with empowering children. And yet here was one of my treasured contacts for this book talking about changing people's behaviour, and hence their attitudes: PSE as control. A newly qualified teacher said to me: 'It's like when a child does a thing really terrible and you ask them why and they don't know why...or they can't express why...'

The question why is interesting, first, because it is asked by teachers who don't want to know the answer. How many times have I said, 'Why are you doing that?' to a child who was, say, rolling rounders balls across the long jump sandpit, or trying to burn a piece of paper with the sun refracted through a school magnifying glass? What is the child supposed to say? 'It's interesting. It's educational. I want to see what happens when...' Secondly, the behaviourist teacher is not concerned with the question 'Why?' applied to any aspect of a child's learning. 'How?' is enough for him or her. This is fine for training in elementary road safety, for example – a necessary part of schooling. But education goes deeper and asks 'Why?'

The newly qualified teacher continued:

You can stop them becoming victims again if you retrain them behaviour-wise...Secret cuddles? I don't teach that bit. What I tend to teach the children is that if they're in a situation where they feel uncomfortable or frightened or any of the other emotions that don't make them feel good...then nobody can tell them to keep it a secret and similarly if someone cuddles them and they want to tell then that's OK...If they want to keep it a secret for some reasons, that's fine, but if they don't want to keep it a secret...and there are problems with that in that children who've been abused their view of things is so distorted...I've talked to adults who remember enjoying abuse...Michele Elliott's beliefs are about empowering children.

I have in front of me as I write Michele Elliott's *Feeling Happy Feeling Safe: A Safety Guide for Young Children*, published by

Hodder and Stoughton. Nothing could be more obvious than the fact that the aims of this book are entirely honourable: to help children to avoid danger from adults. I am a father, so I do not, for all sorts of reasons, want to rubbish anybody's attempts to protect children like my son. So what is it that disturbs me about this book?

In a note for adults at the beginning of the book, Elliott writes

> Children are very touchy, feely little creatures and loving touch is vital for them. They must not be put off touching, but need to learn that it should never be kept secret and they can say no to touches they don't like.

The patronising tone of this is the first worry. My son, I want to exclaim indignantly, is not 'a touchy, feely little creature'. An attitude towards children that can be expressed in such sentimental terms is not only disrespectful, but is also unlikely to lead to autonomous learning. Michele Elliott's beliefs are about empowering touchy, feely little creatures. It simply doesn't fit. Second, the problem with teaching children to say 'No' in circumstances that may harm them is that school, and indeed almost all adult/child relationships – at home, in Brownies and Cubs, in extra-curricular activities – is based on obedience. Elliott herself ackowledges this, without inferring from her story the obvious solution:

> One Mum wrote to me about her three-year-old daughter, who had been abducted while she was in a park with the child. The mother glanced away for a minute, only to look up and see her child being led away by a man. She ran after the abductor, grabbed her daughter back, and rang the police. Then she asked her daughter why she hadn't shouted, as Mum was only yards away. Her daughter had replied that she had started to, but the man said to keep quiet, so she did. *Her instinct for survival had been outweighed by her desire to be obedient* [my italics].

The solution is obvious, though I freely acknowledge it is not simple. We have to find ways of educating our children to be autonomous, and of insisting on their autonomy under provocation. This is going to imply a massive shift in thinking about our relationships with children. This will not be achieved by what is called assertiveness training – nor, indeed, by any other kind of training. For an example of this, we will not teach children to be their own people, to protect their autonomy, by training them to say 'No' to questions like 'Do you like asparagus?' or 'Would you like a dirt sandwich?' Like all training, this merely reinforces behaviour, and does not teach the subtle differences in circumstances, nor take account of the differences in ourselves at different times.

One further problem about the Elliott approach is seen in this sentence: 'We all want to educate children to be alert to danger without depriving them of their innocence'. But children are not innocent. See, for example, the racist attitudes expressed by three-year-olds. Here again sentimentality gets in the way as powerfully as viciousness, to prevent us educating children about the realities of life in the wild that comprises our cities and countryside today.

Keith Waterhouse's novel *There is a Happy Land*, published in 1957, is still one of the most moving and educative books on the subject of sexual violence towards children – in this case adolescents. Reading this novel to my twelve-year-old son, I was struck how Waterhouse reveals *gradually* the horrible truth about what happens to Marion (a sexual murder), which is how children learn about such violence. There is also a moving description, seen from the young boy's point of view, of an aborted but still frightening sexual attack.

Ways of helping children gain autonomy

In my book *The Expressive Arts* I tell a story about a boy suddenly asked, for the sake of his teacher's MA thesis, to say what he thought of a dance lesson caught on video (1993, chapter 6). The boy is inarticulate, because this situation is completely novel to him. Ask me? About this lesson? Why is she doing it? But I can't ask that!:

> 'How would you describe your movements?' [says the teacher]. 'Mostly close together...[replies Christopher]. Some of the time big movements, but most of the time little movements'. 'Is there anything else you'd like to say about it?' 'No, not really'.

We might, as teachers, constantly ask children for their opinions about education, about content and style of lessons, about adults in school and outside. We might put in place systems for finding out about what they think of assemblies, field trips and other school events, so that when they are asked an opinion they are not surprised into silence as Christopher was. This would, first, teach them to question in turn the motives of all adults who, however obscurely, threaten them. I know that this has huge implications about what is commonly called 'discipline' in schools, but how else are we to provide children with the strength to say 'No' with reason, and understanding something of the meaning of the situation? Second, encouraging this kind of conversation will offer us, as teachers, a view of the educational moment seen from the most important point of view, that of the child.

I have argued in chapter 2 that the arts have a capacity to enable comment in a classroom on life and death. It is art that faces up, that follows 'to the bottom of the night' (Auden again, 'In Memory of W. B. Yeats'), that legitimises the illegitimate, that makes temporarily bearable what is unbearable. 'I like a look of agony,/Because I know it's true,' wrote Emily Dickinson. Certainly this sometimes brings about risks of embarrassment or distress.

Frank Smith (*Writing and the Writer*, 1982) says that 'writing can rearrange the past. This is one reason that writing can be such a learning experience'. He, no doubt, had in his mind the power Stalin, Hitler and other tyrants used (and still use) to change history. But the innocent, too, can interfere with time if they only learn to use language effectively. And if we can rearrange the past with words on the page, it must be a powerful tool for learning. Perhaps as we read children poems, or play them music, or show them pictures and dance, we are helping them rearrange the future. Perhaps we are helping them to protect themselves, to be strong. 'How much,' wrote John Danby in his 1940 book *Approach to Poetry*, 'adult behaviour is a stale attempt at going over again in actuality what has been gone over before – much more richly – in play or phantasy or fiction?...the adult behaviour [is] the bit of plagiarism...'

If we are not timid in our choice of art for children – if we read them Blake, and current picture books about death (John Burningham's *Grandpa*, for example, and Alice Walker's *To Hell with Dying* (referred to in chapter 2)); if we allow them to play with danger mentally, spiritually and emotionally when they are young – there is a possibility that we will make the threatening situation in the park a mere plagiarism, and they will have the power of will to do the safe, imaginative thing. In giving children this power over texts about birth, love and death, we are giving them power for later on when the three essential facts of our common humanity not only excite and thrill us, but threaten us with loneliness and, finally, extinction.

Getting children talking about texts in groups after reading them is one way of giving them this power. Here is an extract from a transcript of a group of eight-year-olds talking, without their teacher's presence, after reading together 'Anne and the Field-Mouse' by Ian Serraillier (from Sedgwick, 'Getting it true: Notes on the teaching of poetry', in *Curricula for Diversity in Education* Tony Booth *et al* 1992). At the end of the poem Serraillier's children, having watched a mouse frightened by a pheasant, chalk '...in capitals on a rusty can:/THERE'S A MOUSE IN THOSE NETTLES. LEAVE/HIM ALONE. NOVEMBER 15th. ANNE.'

LISA One day I was, um, outside when there was a load of lizards down the bottom of our garden. And a worm came up and slithered over one...

JOHN Right. Have you ever seen, say if your cat hit a bird, have you ever seen it?

IAN (*largely inaudible*) Cat...bird...porch...

JOAN One day, my mum hates birds, right, so my cat, um, um, killed one and brought it indoors and my mum screamed and my da- my brother had to pick it up and take it outside.

JOHN Have you ever buried an animal?

ANN You've said that!

JOHN I've got to talk about it. Have you...

(*Long pause*)

JOHN Have you ever...put them in...buried the animal yourself?...

Children rarely have sufficient opportunities to talk without the teacher's presence. In this short extract, we see the apparently sturdy John (who has, in effect, chaired the meeting throughout) struggling through to the expression of his anxiety about the death and burial of animals. This was after much chat and jockeying for position. We have to risk that chat and that jockeying for such possible coming to terms with things. We also have to risk silences: arguably, the most potent emotional and intellectual activity happening here happens during the stage direction *Long pause*. How can what occurs mentally and emotionally in these silences be measured? Will all such occurrences be reflected in observable behaviour? We know from our lives that they will not, that we have often reflected on, for example, our relationships, without enacting our reflections.

Talking in small groups about anything, without the supervising presence of a teacher, is educational because it is heuristic. That is, it helps children to set up possibilities, and to knock them down, and to set up new ones. It helps them negotiate meanings, both linguistic and social. It helps them proceed by trial and error. In other words, it helps them learn for themselves. And if you learn for yourself, you learn more purposefully than if you learn for someone else, be it teacher, examiner, parent or employer. And the presence of an adult contaminates the process as s/he all too readily short-circuits learning with his/her interventions. This is (I am told) similar to the contaminating presence of a man, however sympathetic, in a women's group, or (rather less critically) an education tutor in a staffroom, as teachers talk about changing their practice (see chapter 7). The power of individuals to grasp autonomy for themselves depends on their ability to proceed in groups without the powerful outsider.

Thea Prisk, in her article 'Letting them get on with it: a study of unsupervised talk in an infant school' (in Andrew Pollard's 1987 book, *Children and their Primary Schools*), says: 'Teacher-dominated talk...cannot help pupils to acquire all the social and communicative skill important for the future educational development.' One might add here that such talk will also get in the way of children discovering ways of making themselves safe. Here are four eight-year-olds talking without the presence of an adult. They have read an account of a child being abducted in a public park:

MARTIN Would you have gone off?
JIMMY NO!
CLARE No. And I like *(inaudible)*
JENNY Yeah. When she went off, she must've thought –
MARTIN She must've thought –
  Long pause
JENNY She was gonna get sweets and things, an' she must've thought –
  Long pause
MARTIN What happened to her?
JIMMY He did something bad to her –
JENNY He touched her...

Of course there is an ethical (and therefore PSME) issue here. Should we be eavesdropping on these children, who had been told nothing about the tape recorder? It is probably better to tell them about the machine and live with the problems of self-consciousness that this brings about.

Children exploring their anger and violence through writing

Exploring children's feelings of anger is a way of seeing into their lives, and of allowing them to express themselves:

When I was angrey mummy woodet Let me play on my sega and I tride to get my own way. When it is bed time I say sory mummy then she ses tats arit my sasig (That's all right, my sausage]

my bruf pols my her it fils lik I am getting a hed ak and I hit my bruf bak and when my mummy sey I cut't hava a pis of bred and in sid I fil pike [pink]

When I am angry my Bortha colls me a peg and I fill horde [horrible] and my face goes all red with agea and I poose him in the Buth and tone the tap on foll blrst and I fill all red but then I sory and diy [dry] his coves [clothes]

These children are 6 years old. With older children, I sometimes read Vasco Popa's poem from *Junior Voices* 4 'Give Me Back My Rags', which is about the anger we all feel at a friend at some time or another. Blake's poem 'A Poison Tree' explores the same emotions:

I was angry with my friend:
I told my wrath, my wrath did end.
I was angry with my foe:
I told it not, my wrath did grow.

And I water'd it in fears,
Night and morning with my tears;
And I sunned it with smiles,
And with soft deceitful wiles.

And it grew both day and night,
Till it bore an apple bright;
And my foe beheld it shine,
And he knew that it was mine,

And into my garden stole
When the night had veil'd the pole:
In the morning glad I see
My foe outstretched beneath the tree.

Then I ask them to explore these feelings:

I cared for you, but no more.
I'll smash your tiny cottage door.
I scrape you with thorns and then
I'll make your hands bleed and bleed again.

I'll smash your face in and kill your father
But your mother, I won't harm her.
With my ears I will tear your clothes to rags.
I will tie you into lots of bags.

I have in my possession a painting, in powder paints on large sugar paper, of a face in strong colours. Indeed, the paper is covered in deep reds, blues, and yellows. It is reproduced in *Drawing to Learn* (Sedgwick and Sedgwick 1993) where we give this account of its creation:

> The teacher praised this piece as she felt it deserved recognition, but when she went back to the girl the CND-shaped symbol had been dragged down the face. The teacher told us: "I said, 'Why have you done that?' and she just burst into tears and ran out of the room. Much later it emerged she'd been bullied and I think this picture is about that bullying in some way..." This is as eloquent an example as we could hope for to show how art contributes to our work in PSE. The girl used normal communication skills (words) to tell her story but it was her art that opened the floodgates and which brought about the expression.

Paul was a boy with a problem with his temper. He would fly into rages at the smallest crossing of his will, on the playground, in the classroom, and elsewhere. Once he was asked to write a poetic version of a passage of prose which had, in turn, been worked from a poem, Stephen Spender's 'My parents kept me from children who were rough' (idea from Sandy Brownjohn's *What rhymes with secret?*; the poem can be found in many anthologies):

I feared more than those
  bizarre animals
    those mysterious
      sounds
    were
    unfriendly

they were foul-mouthed
  and they
  glanced at me
    wildly
they wore fragments
    of torn velvet

I was invisible through the
  remote lakes I was
  trying to act scarce

In Smith and Thompson's 1991 book, *Practical Approaches to Bullying* there are several innovative suggestions for using art as a way to understand, if not counteract, violence. Angela M. Horton's account of the use of *The Heartstone Odyssey* is one example, and Francis Gobey describes a practical approach through drama. Gobey points out that

> A class discussion rarely gets much further than...some people are bullies, some are victims, some are neither, that is the way things are...*Drama* [his italics] *can help to extend and deepen an agreed definition of bullying...can establish that behaviour is to a certain extent a matter of choice.* Just as an actor tries out a role, so can workshop participants try out different sorts of behaviour...

So can all the arts:

My brain said stop! but I did'nt. I tried to think but my brain couldn't think. I tried to keep calm but it didn't work. Horrible demolished legs. It is great to kick people. My friends gathered around her. I was in charge now. I can do what I want...

Work of this kind helps children to generalise their experience of bullying until they understand it in the context of the society in which they live. It helps them practice the look of agony which, in the mixture that their lives will be, will inevitably have its place. And to patronise them as feeling little innocents, or to sentimentalise their world as one in which we mustn't mention violence by its name in art, is to sell them short.

CHAPTER FIVE

Replacement radiators and flower smashers: talking about gender

> We don't have a problem with gender here. We make sure the girls play with the lego and get time on the computer, but however much you encourage them, they prefer not to use construction toys...

> We've found it's no problem, we've gone past work on gender. We're all equal here! The girls do what they want!

The first speaker was the headteacher of a school where the staff had 'based the entire curriculum on PSME'. In many ways she and the second teacher – a year five leader in a middle school – were typical of many whom I talked to in the researching and writing of this book. To use the title of Chris Gain's useful text on racism, they represent the 'No Problem Here' constituency: We've cracked bullying in our school, there is no racial discrimination, boys and girls are equal. 'Everything is All Right,' as Mary Jane Drummond puts it in her article, 'Learning about gender in primary schools' in Peter Lang's book *Thinking about Personal and Social Education in the Primary School* – even as

> Groups of fifth form and sixth form pupils from the next door comprehensive came regularly to work in the school: [but] why had we done nothing when we noticed the fifth form group (the much-despised CSE 'homemakers') were all girls? [and]...*One Two Three and Away*, the reading scheme we'd used to replace *Through the Rainbow*, was every bit as unbalanced as the notorious Ladybird Readers...

The second remark at the beginning of this chapter has the implication 'as far as that's possible'. These observations have characteristics in common with a comment made by a teacher in a village in Norfolk, where I was working with teachers on the Jewish festival Hannakah: 'This may be all right in King's Lynn, but we don't have any Jews around here'. As teachers we have ways of making sure that questions about certain subjects don't crop up. We conceal issues about justice by telling ourselves that problems do not exist – and if they do, they are the responsibility, not of ourselves, but of others, the parents, or even the children. 'The attitudes they bring to school are wrong,' we say. 'And anyway the girls won't play with the construction toys'.

We can look with interested attention at one of these schools, the middle – and there appears, indeed, at first sight, to be no problem. Between lessons, little knots of children stand around in the entrance hall. Some are mixed in sex, some are single sex. Boys and girls comment to each other about work, about television. A teacher emerges from the staffroom and talks to Roy and Lisa about something in his last lesson with them, and as I watch in my nervous voyeuristic manner I can see no difference in the way he speaks to them. But 'The spirit of justice and truth is nothing else but a certain kind of attention,' as Simone Weil says, and this attention has to be more than interested. It has to be 'intense ...*dis*interested...generous' (Weil again). So I keep watching.

Later in the classroom the children – eleven-year-olds – make a point of sitting separately. The register is divided by sex. In an hour, the children have drafted riddles, and I ask them to pick out classmates to guess the answer to each riddle, and without exception, boys choose boys and girls girls. When you meet pairs of children on messages around the school, the couples are always single-sex. On the playground, again the sexes are divided, apart from a small group of children on the edge, by the dining hall, who swap banter about current hit music, *Take That* and *Guns 'n' Roses*.

Another PSME-oriented school sent me similar comments on gender. The headteacher said:

> None of us is ultra-feminist here, but there are certain feminist strands, certain feminine styles of management...the children don't have assertive male models, even the caretaker is a woman. As for teaching jobs, the men aren't good enough...At home round here the man is often unemployed and the mothers are often out to work on shifts and of course they [the mothers] are not in at tea-time, and the men, who *are* there, because they've got no job, they lack the skills that the women have built up over a generation and their care is

shallow, it's bodily care only, and then, when she's finished at work, the mother comes in, and she does what she did before...

This passage, placing the issue of the way we define gender in schools in the context of deprivation, unemployment and injustice sent me spinning. First there was the apologetic 'None of us is ultra-feminist...' It is still necessary to make obeisance to male hegemony when you are questioned, even about this subject. We are not *ultra*-feminist. Then there was the conflation of feminine with female. To be in power as women is still to face problems about what male power calls 'feminine', as though gaining autonomy as females depends on feminity.

Then there was the perceived fact: men aren't good enough at teaching to get jobs here. This is evidently largely true. There are far fewer men than women in primary schools. But despite this, in one town I know, twenty-two of the primary headteachers are men, fifteen women. The picture is far worse nationally. And, of course, of those women, six are heads of infant schools, as though women aren't as capable of running primary or junior schools. These facts, which represent the state of affairs in most of the United Kingdom, place our work as teachers concerned with justice in schools against a background of institutionalised injustice.

There was in this headteacher's words the implication of men being suddenly out of work. Here the comments introduce the economic realities of family life. The skills that the men possessed, and even rejoiced in, are now no use, because they have lost their jobs. The men, in an important sense, are emasculated. Because their definition was as a member of a workplace, they are defined as ready for the scrapheap, both by themselves and by society. They are also not much good at what women can do, at what generations of women, through the agency of male oppression, have learned to do. These men can't bring up children; can only care for them 'bodily'...And thus women are even more repressed than before, having two jobs, as many, indeed, have had for years.

One frequently hears examples of sexist attitudes and practice by men in teaching. And I put these in a context as well: 'I spent two hundred pounds on her, so why shouldn't I do what I did?' a convicted rapist is reported to have said to a police officer. An affliction, a crime, exists in this man's mind purely as a financial statistic. My context here is, first, how men talk about and behave towards women, and, second – and this is true of all this book – how human beings are defined managerially today as statistics (see, for a devastating critique of management, Stephen J Ball's article 'Management as moral technology' in his book *Foucault and education* (Routledge, 1990).

> It's all gone too far, we are the oppressed sex now...Girls don't need f otball training, their skills are different, they're better at other aspects of games...Let's face it, girls are better at writing, they just are, boys are better at things like maths and physics...I know we're not supposed to say things like this, but [playful slap on his own wrist] there are these basic differences between men and women...

The first of these remarks (all culled from staffrooms in the south-east) is in part facetious, but it is also said at times when supposed sexist remarks are made by women about men. Indeed, it is now, in staffrooms, acceptable for women to make jokey-lascivious comments about men in a way in which it is unacceptable the other way round. But men inherit centuries of hegemony which give their remarks power. Women making similar remarks take on only the power of a *riposte*. Nevertheless, when a woman like the pop star Madonna produces what by all acounts is a book of soft pornography, and in so doing 'expresses her sexuality', it seems inconsistent to say the least (and hypocritical to say rather more) to condemn sexual responses to that book as uniformly sexist.

The second remark above, about the football skills, is disingenuous because these men never mention in this context that the parts of games, or the games themselves, that girls are supposedly better at are never the parts that have any prestige. So this argument again reinforces the power of a male-run society.

Many teachers actively reinforce false gender roles: 'Can I have six big strong boys, please...?' is still heard, despite the fact that girls at this age are just as strong as boys. Registers are still divided in terms of sex, and the going in and coming out of classrooms is organized in groups made up of girls – first, usually – and then boys. And all this happens after pre-school experiences during which, as Hilary Minns says ('Girls don't have holes in their clothes' in *Alice in Genderland* NATE 1985) 'children's sex-role behaviour is well established before they come to school'. In the same article, Minns quotes books found in many schools that teach boys and girls clearly defined behaviour. Schools, one might argue, have a duty to break these stereotypical notions down, to help children to face up to what happens when we look beyond the surface into the dark where we are individuals. Instead, it's 'six big strong boys please...'

Ideas that almost always provoke disagreement are inherently more educational than others. This is partly because these ideas are, by their nature, at the heart of our living, and partly because, as Socrates and Jesus Christ evidently knew, education proceeds by reflection, argument (or collaborative enquiry) and action. 'Without Contraries is no progression', as Blake says. Through controversy we learn. This is true of each of the critical issues with which this book is concerned: justice, love, sex, death, violence, racism, and, of course, in the present instance, discrimination. But despite (or indeed, possibly because of) the educational possibility inherent in controversy, we fly from such curricular issues, and pretend all is well.

In schools, I have found little discussion of the issue that I (inadvertently) made arise in one school. I asked a group of 10-year-old boys in a single sex preparatory school to write kennings. Sandy Brownjohn writes about this form in her book *The Ability to Name Cats* (1989). 'A kenning,' she tells me in a letter, 'was an Old Norse technique used in writing or storytelling which was a new descriptive name, usually two words, based on an attribute of the original; for example, "swan's way" for the sea, or "Beo-wulf" – the enemy (wolf) of the bee, i.e. a bear...children concentrate their minds on the subject and produce phrases which will combine to build up a picture of it'.

A boy, Alec, wrote 'Music':

A pleasure-Maker,
A happiness-giver,
A mood-changer,
A meditation-sanctifier,
The Phantom of the Opera's friend,
The organist's delight,
The Devil's delight,
A musician's delight,
An ear-splitting glass shatterer,
A bad mood Mum Maker,
A sudden explosion of beautiful sound,
An anti-dull sound bomb.

At the end of this exercise, I suggested that the boys might write kennings on the subject 'Girls'. This may have been a sexist act in itself. Throw this idea in at the end of a session? OK lads, here's a subject? It didn't feel like that at the time. Either way, what happened next surprised and dismayed all of us – visiting writer and three teachers, one male and two female. The sheer vigour and inventiveness of the following examples deepened my dismay; these were obviously attitudes and beliefs that were rooted strongly in these boys' minds. Later, I showed the work to other teachers. I suppose all of us assumed that something in the admittedly fragile liberal/intellectual ethos of our times would have moderated some of the extremes of ignorance and chauvinism that boys would show in classroom work to be read by at least four teachers. We were wrong:

Girls
A bedtime enjoyment
A heartthrob
A love-letter sender
A replacement radiator
A lipstick leaver
A walking gas perfume bomb
A sanity slasher
A double bed proposition
A child bringer
A life bond
An adrenalin pumper
A total knackerer

A boys dream.
A diamond's best friend.
A mad shopper.
A fashion hopper.
A bikini buyer.
A tight weaver.
A strawberry tart.

Target practice
Take That lover
Hair perfecter
Cindy Crawford admirer
Spotty Grotty
A perfume ponger

These were typical of the boys' responses. They seemed to be more conscious of sex than their age would have led us to anticipate, and nearly all the boys seemed to see girls in either sexual or providing terms (one definition was 'kitchen-hopper') or as child-rearers. There was a hint of girls as dangerous, too, in the most dramatically chauvinistic of all the responses: 'A total knackerer'. These boys were not clowning. They settled down to the task with relish: 'Yeah!' they chorused when I suggested the subject, and they produced these poems without any conversation among themselves. There was, therefore, no collusion. Only very rarely was there a response which I would have called boyish, a reaction from Richmal Crompton's William books: 'spotty grotty' or 'perfume ponger'; the kind of response to which it would have been possible, if questionable, to attach the word 'innocent'.

They were learning as they wrote about their feelings for their sisters, mothers and female friends; and in the discussion that would have taken place had there been time they would have learned about other views on this controversial issue. They were exposing the degree to which they were influenced by the world of the television advertisement ('Hair perfecter', 'Bikini buyer'). More seriously, they might have fruitfully discussed the extent to which they had exposed fear and ignorance and budding delusions of power and supremacy.

I think, in passing, that the teachers at this school must be complimented on having developed an ethos in which such views can be so readily and vigorously expressed. The question of whether such views are dominant in the class which sends its boys to single sex private schools is a difficult one, and probably one which this chapter will only nervously skirt. What is certain is that you cannot realise an equal opportunities policy in a single sex school. Whatever high-minded policies a staff might develop in such a school, the boys (in this case) have no chance to practise those policies. They have, in Bronwyn Davies's terms (1989), no opportunities to learn discursive practices that are not almost entirely male-biased. While it is often true that in all girl schools girls have greater opportunities in areas of the curriculum that are traditionally male-dominated, the price paid for this is the lack of experiences through which the sexes are able to explore ways of treating each other as human beings, not solely as girls and boys.

The rest of my time in this town was spent in the girls' prep school nearby, where some of the girls were sisters of the boys. The obvious thing to do was to get the girls to write kennings about the boys. The first task went as well as it had with the boys.

For example:

Sun
A smile maker,
A happiness brightener,
A clothes fader,
A playing whirlpool,
A hot machine,
A bright churner,
A kind likener,
A sad burning,
A mood changer,
A child's delight,
The world's happiness.

Rain
A flood flame
A spitting swiper
A flowing drizel
A colour blender
A wet welly
A pouring drip
A puddle player
A holiday destroyer

And then I suggested kennings about boys. Again, the girls responded with gusto. I could hardly wait to see what they'd write, and went around looking over their shoulders. Here are four complete examples:

A pain in the neck
A prison-filler
A girl's enemy
A dancing maniac
A loser at cards
An unimaginative thing
A flower smasher
A slithery snake

A heart breaker.
A noisy headache.
A love churner.
A hate machine.
A cruel kicker.
Mean with words.
Awful romantics.
A fiersome fighter.
Nasty and naughty.
A staring lover.

An idle bonehead.
A scatterbrain.
A careless driver.
A telephone book.

A dollop of mud
A girl's doom or not?
A money spender
A green muddy warty fat toad
A thing to be thrown away

A spotty blob
An immature brat
A girl's galore
A ball of mud
A heart breaker
A waist [*sic*] of time

While largely negative, the girls' responses are very different from the boys, being rooted mostly in a school story, puppy-dogs' tails country where boys are are dirty, ugly and rough. This is the equivalent of 'spotty grotty' and 'perfume ponger' in the boys' work. Very few of the boys wrote in these quasi-innocent 'boyish' terms, while most of the girls were, I suppose, 'girlish'. They responded as a less precious Violet Elizabeth Bott might have done. My friend comments, 'These are from *Woman's Own*/Georgette Heyer fiction of the 1950s. What*ever* do girls read under their desks these days?'

There are other hints, though: 'prison-filler', 'loser at cards' and 'careless driver' anticipate, possibly somewhat melodramatically (but no less disturbingly for that), adult tragedy. And the romance is there even though the sex is far less blunt than with the boys: 'heart breaker', 'love churner', 'awful romantics'. Other examples of this were 'kind kisser', 'hansom person' and 'a girl's love'. In sum, I would suggest that the girls are more subtle, more uncertain of their point of view – or perhaps they are simply more honest and more ambivalent: a girl's doom or not? They are readier than the boys to accept the uncertainty, the ambivalence, of sexual relationships.

On the way home, I resolved to try the same experiment in classes of 10-year-old children in mixed schools to see if I could see any differences. I also sent copies of this material to various colleagues and friends. Sandy Brownjohn read most of the above, and her response was innocent of gender issues:

The girls are usually more mature than boys at these ages and this may account for the slightly more subtle approach, but maybe both are just more honest, as children generally are, than adults who put a veneer of sophistication on any public utterances about the opposite sex. In private they may still conform to the primeval instincts which are probably always going to be just below the surface. The sexual drive and 'competition' between the sexes is such a basic instinct that the civilising aspects of modern society may only ever paper over them...

In other words, for Brownjohn, adults conceal – to return to a recurring theme in this book – understandings of their primeval instincts, while these ten-year-olds have simply been frank about those instincts. Indeed, a more civilised response, to use a word from Brownjohn, in which the boys had referred to the girls as human beings and not almost exclusively *sexual/providing* human beings would, for Brownjohn, have been a weaker response. For her, 'bedtime enjoyment', 'strawberry tart', 'unimaginative thing' and 'flower smasher' are simply evidence of honesty. I am reminded of an occasion when, as a sixth former, I complained to an English teacher that D. H. Lawrence's characters were always struggling for supremacy, men 'extinguishing' women (George and Meg in *The White Peacock*), women defeating men (Anna and Will in *The Rainbow*). The teacher said that Lawrence was merely being honest. 'Wait till you're married...'

So is the feminist response to these poems another sentimental concealment? Sex is, after all, central to most of us. But to describe each other almost entirely as sex objects is to be, as my friend put it earlier, 'not very respectful', and individuals in a semi-public setting have a role to play socially that precedes a sexual one. Concentration on a predatory view of the other sex (and that is what emerges from the boys' writing) is evidence of potential danger. This may be the key: perhaps boys fear girls as danger-ous, while ten-year-old girls know that boys aren't dangerous – yet: just a bit muddy. All this work is cause for us to think about how we teach children to define themselves and other people.

A class of mixed ten-year-olds in a primary school in York gave me the first opportunity to compare attitudes as expressed through this exercise. This school was a contrast to the prep schools in several ways: the children were in a state school; they were, almost certainly, less well-off (although there was little evidence of poverty on the children's faces and in their clothing);

and they were grouped in mixed sex classes.

It has to be said that there was no evidence in the boys' writing of the kind of crude, powerfully-expressed chauvinism found in the single sex class. A few examples show again that note of fear:

A boy's nightmare
A boy's night of hell
A girl on her own makes a boy scream
A boy's nadir...

Some were largely neutral or even affectionate and praising:

A skirt-wearer
A master [*sic*] at netball
A skilled sew
A user of hairbands
An arguer and a battler
The opposite to men
A little women [*sic*]

Some combined neutrality with a determined even-handedness:

A different person than a boy
A boy's disaster
A boy's delight
A person who wears lots of make-up
A person with a high voice
A person you go out with
A person you dump
A person who plays different games

The only chauvinist line by a boy was 'a sexual disaster' – and who is to say this isn't more about the boy's own fears than about girls? It was embedded in a poem otherwise largely 'William the Bad' in tone:

A boys hell
A sexual disaster
A bad smell
A teachers pet
A whimpish soul
A mothers hell
A parents nightmare
A picture of love
A boys despise

The girls, on the whole, raised the matter of sex more than the boys – albeit in innocent enough ways: 'A lipstick smudger...A lips delight...', but the most delightful of all the poems simply saw boys from the point of view of practically every member of the family. Even though one can see here certain gender-oriented battle lines being drawn up, there is genuine observation and a disarming honesty; an utter lack of a frantic will to amuse peers and teachers which is observable nearly everywhere else in this data:

Boy's

A Dad's delight.

A Mum's Headace.

A uncle's follower.

A Aunts enemy.

A Grandads mate.

A Grandma's cuddly toy.

A Sisters Hitting toy.

A Brothers rage.

For Brownjohn, these children are, presumably, suppressing knowledge of primeval instincts. And, indeed, these poems are less powerful than the poems written by the boys in the single sex school. Like Milton's Satan, the devil in this case evidently has the best tunes – if you like power. Or, more likely, the ethos of the mixed school, which encouraged girls to take part in activities traditionally reserved for boys; which did not distinguish girls from boys administratively; in which games were played together – it may be that this ethos had led to more generous, loving, attentive attitudes.

In Bronwyn Davies's terms (*Frogs and Snails and Feminist Tales*, 1989), we have to go further back and ask how, as individuals, we become male or female. Davies insists that children are not passive receivers of socialisation; that, in contrast, they contribute to their socialisation to the point where the term is inappropriate. 'The words are bipolar, the people are not'. A male hegemony disadvantages girls in many ways – as Jackson, quoted in Davies, puts it,

> ...if we teach children that it is indecent to reveal their underwear, and then proceed to dress half of them in skirts, we are placing that half at a distinct disadvantage.

Certainly, the children at the single sex schools were more restricted by their clothes than the children in the non-uniform state school where the sexes mixed freely. Davies gives examples of both boys and girls in pre-schools adopting clothes to help them change situations, and the girls in many state schools are allowed to wear trousers. My twelve-year-old son says that none of his 'friends who are girls wear skirts unless they have to'. Opportunities to express preferences were completely denied the uniformed children at the single sex schools. Neither the girls nor the boys had any opportunity to position themselves discursively as male or female, or to take up what Bronwyn Davies calls 'multiple positionings'.

Eight year 6 children wrote first drafts of poems about domestic jobs as though they were a man or a woman doing that job. I am not dealing with second drafts because, as I write, I am two weeks from my deadline. For the same reason, I am not able to discuss what the children would say about each other's writing.

We would have seen learning in this conversation: how do they relate to points of view and experiences that are foreign to their own? What is happening in the gaps between points made in a discussion? How would the boys relate to the evident despair in some of the girls' writing? And how would the girls feel about some of the boys' jokes?

What follows, then, might ideally be an account of these discussions. But it is mostly made up of extracts from the initial drafts:

Washing The Dishes

Picking up the dishes with no washing
gloves on,
Feeling the cheese sauce, slither between
my fingers.
Putting my hands into the water with
pasta floating in it,
And thinking about the 10 plates
I have to do next.

Having to scrub the plates which were
used for the curry,
Looking into the coffee cup where
the stains of coffee lie,
Making sure I don't cut myself
with the large kitchen knife,
Building up the courage to
look into the pot which was used for
the bolognese.

Ailsa

Uh-oh, the kids' room,
How come the wife always leaves *me* to wipe up all the spilt drinks
I wish I could be at the pub having a pint of bitter.
Why do they always have to put the bits of lego
Under the lowest chair they can find?
Oh no, they've been eating doughnuts again and guess where the jam
goes...

Christopher

Here I am having been up all night with the baby,
Holding a duster and a can of polish,
Picking up the ornaments,
Finding somewhere to put them,
Moving the pile of books on the table so I can put down the can of polish,
Why should I be doing this.
Why not my husband?
Oh, and there's the baby crying again
And over goes the clothes horse with all the clean washing
And I've still got to phone that shop to tell them that our tumble dryer
doesn't work.

Anna

Oh no, the wife has gone to a meeting, leaving me to do all the ironing...I don't even know how to switch the iron on. I think I'm supposed to put the plug in and switch the socket on. Hold it! She always puts water in the iron. Just pour the water in nice and slowly...Bzzzzzzzz, ahhhhhhh, help meeeeeee...I'd better go up stairs, my hair is standing on end...

Andrew

I've got to do the living room dusting the lot while him Brian sits on his throne watching the last match of the world cup and he won't budge off the sofa for me to tidy under there. Oh no in come the children going on about that match between Manchester City and Liverpool. Oh what could be worse football conversations all around me...His majesty just sits there watching the match...

Kerry

The boys tended to make the exercise into a joke: 'the wife' (twice), 'at the pub having a pint of bitter' and 'guess where the jam goes' are pure downmarket sitcom. In this way the boys, writing independently and not colluding, nevertheless close ranks to conceal the central issue. And, we might say, *'the'* wife is not very respectful.

The pieces that ring true were by girls: that they had done some of the work described is clear from the vivid details, the way they use all the senses, especially in Ailsa's poem ('Feeling the cheese sauce slither between my fingers,/Putting my hands into the water with pasta floating in it'), and also from the rhythms of their writing. It is striking how Ailsa's poem has no main verb – often a fault in children's writing, as they work to avoid the kind of commitment that a main verb brings, but here the succession of present participles – 'Picking up...Feeling... Putting...thinking...Having to...Looking...Making...Building' – provides a breathless implicit description of the round of domestic tasks.

Children offered opportunities to write like this, and then to discuss their words in small groups, are being given chances to see the sexes as something infinitely less bipolar than replacement radiators and flower smashers. Through the writing and the talk, they can explore the infinite variety that is being human. They can see that we divide in far more complex ways than simply by sex, and they can transcend the bigotries of a previous generation.

CHAPTER SIX

Combating racism

The question is, in the classroom, is it legal to be racist?

letter from a nurse

Racism was not an issue whilst growing up in Dominica. I was not in the minority there. It wasn't until I came to England that I found my colour was a problem to some people...I also noticed that the children at my school were not taking education as seriously as we were brought up to do in Dominica.

Paula Sorhaindo

Before I say anything about racism in schools, I want to look again at the context in which I write, and in which you read. Listening to Woman's Hour in the car on the way back from Cavell First School (see chapter 1), I found a gross example of racism. Black fashion models talked about their difficulty in getting work. One said of a photographer: 'He told me I was lovely, very European...then he asked me if I'd had plastic surgery'. The manager of an agency for black models said that it was 'a fact of life' that black models who weren't really black, who were olive-skinned, found work easier to come by. Later, reading Toni Morrison's *Playing in the Dark*, I found this distinction again. In her analysis of Willa Cather's novel *Sapphira and the slave girl*, Morrison notes the difference between the light-skinned heroine, Nancy, and the 'the dark-skinned "field" niggers'. What would be an analagous distinction between groups of whites?

On the Woman's Hour programme an advertiser said that, if he used too many black models, white women would feel that 'my product wasn't for them'. Being black in our society is not analagous to being white in it. Being white isn't an issue. Being black always is.

A *Guardian* diary entry (1994) tells us about three famous young footballers standing, smart-suited, on a London street after an official function. Two are black and one is white. But they can't get a taxi until the two black men hide in a shop doorway and the white man flags down a cab on his own.

The 'compliment' paid to a black model because she was 'European-looking'; three young men, two black, one white, trying to get a taxi at night – this is part of the racist context in which teachers and children in schools teach and learn.

As Geoffrey Short and Bruce Carrington observe in Andrew Pollard's book *Children in their Primary Schools* (1987), 'schools in all white areas...have tended to eschew both...multicultural education and anti-racist education'. Indeed, I've seen few schools where I can imagine myself as a black or Asian girl feeling at home. The images on the walls welcome males first, and white males second. The music marching children into assembly (should I get that far) is exclusively white/male. There's plenty of Mozart, Elgar and Tchaikovsky. There's very little Bessie Smith or Billie Holiday, though occasionally there's a touch of Joplin. On the walls there are no Asian images, or if there are any at all, they seem to be of flooded rice fields or of the effects of hurricanes. In my local Indian restaurant (which is, in fact, like most in my area, Bengali) there is a scene of a wide river, on either side of which is rich vegetation: greens of all shades and bright flowers. It has a caption: Beautiful Bangladesh. Children in schools rarely see images like this.

Short and Carrington sum up the differences between multicultural education and anti-racism like this:

> Whereas multiculturalists are principally concerned to celebrate cultural diversity, overcome curricular ethnocentrism, and increase intergroup tolerance, anti-racists stress the need for schools to play a more active role in combating forms of racism at an institutional as well as an individual level. They also advocate fundamental reappraisal of both the formal and hidden curriculum and insist that all schools teach about racism and take steps to promote racial equality and justice.

However, multiculturalism is powerful educationally because it offers choice. As Robert Jeffcoate puts it in *Ethnic Minorities and Education*, 1984:

> The proper aim of a multi-ethnic curriculum is not...to prescribe the attitudes children ought to develop towards their own and other cultures (distorting content choice accordingly). Rather the aim is to provide children with the knowledge and skills to come to a critical understanding of the different cultures impinging upon them, so that they can decide for themselves which cultures, or parts of cultures, are worthy of admiration, allegiance and adoption. A multi-ethnic curriculum should enable them to answer for themselves the fundamental question: How shall I live?

In their defence of anti-racist education, Short and Carrington quote extensively from studies that show incipient racism as early as three years of age. With support from Roland King (*All Things Bright and Beautiful*, 1979) and others, they suggest that progressivism, with its belief in childhood innocence, and its Piagetian notions about readiness, works against anti-racism: are the children *ready* for abstract concepts? Surely children are colour-blind? Short and Carrington view progressivism as ultimately sentimental and, therefore, like all sentimentalities, destructive of our attempts to come to terms with the way things are.

However, a parent was not being sentimental when he said to me:

> We wanted him to grow up among different people...it sounds idealistic, I know, but we wanted him to be a citizen of the world, not of a little white community in a little white town with little white values...

And another parent who had moved to rural Norfolk from South London, and who felt her children 'missed out' because they no longer met Asian or Caribbean children, wasn't either.

But we get a different picture from a recent case where a white child's singing of Pakistani songs was considered a deprivation by her parents, rather than an advantage. Eventually, the local authority agreed to move the child to a school where white faces predominated. This is probably the view held by many white parents. One – a secretary in a school with many Asian and Afro-Caribbean children – told me:

> I wouldn't like him to sing Pakistani songs, there's no need, I know you've got to have the children in your schools, but there's no need for learning their language...He's not going to use it...You can get on with them without learning the songs...

There isn't much chance of missing the racism in those remarks: 'them' (them and us) makes it clear. It is also a common line among some ethnic minorities. 'I send her to an English school because I want her to have an English education. She will get her ethnic culture at home...' That view was put to me several times by Asian parents, while, on the other hand, some Asians want separate schools for their children.

I asked an advisory teacher for multicultural education what you should say to white parents who don't want their child to have a multi-ethnic education – who, at the lowest level of provision, don't want them singing Pakistani songs, or cooking curries, or discovering Divali; who, at a higher one, don't want them learning about the black and Asian experience of colonialism. He told me about an incident where a support teacher taught children Punjabi songs.

> A parent came storming in, objecting, why is my daughter coming home with all this Indian rubbish?...The head pointed to the dear old National Curriculum, the original English document: 'It should be the duty of all teachers to instil in their pupils a civilised respect for other languages...' What better way to do that than singing songs in other languages? This may seem rather legalistic but it's a start...Also, singing a song is sharing experiences. I wonder if people would object to children singing French songs, *Sur le Pont d'Avignon, Frère Jacques,* all that...I would have to ask, why do people feel threatened? there's a race element, there's prejudice, I'm afraid...though one can be too pessimistic...some parents are seeing the value...

Also, of course, singing the songs of other ethnic groups goes a small way to giving confidence to the members of those groups, and it is the job of teachers to encourage all children, to make them what Joan Webster at Cavell First School (see chapter 1) calls 'rising stars'. This might not satisfy parents, whether their racism is nervy and slightly guilty, or whether it is rampant – but a professional obligation is always a first line of defence. 'We teach these songs because it's our duty to *all* the children...Take your worries to the LEA office': not a pretty answer, but an honest and professional one.

The advisory teacher also said:

> It can be fun, if we can still say that in these puritanical times. It helps us celebrate diversity, it gives value to other lives. It gives a sense of achievement...Much of our English chauvinism stems from our attitude to language...that foreigners should speak English. Singing

songs in other languages is useful preparation for secondary school. Why shouldn't language awareness begin at primary level?

Teachers who hear racist comments have a duty to do what they can to counteract them, because we have to teach each other about what respect means. Although, as a teacher in Ipswich said to me, racism-awareness among teachers has grown enormously over the last few years, the real problem still comes with *teachers* who are prejudiced. One 11-year-old English-born Bangladeshi I know is convinced his teachers are racist. 'If you don't do your homework and you're black, you get detention...if you're white you don't...'

One hypocritical expression of racism is the teacher correcting him/herself for a disrespectful comment about black people, and then jokingly slapping him/herself on the wrist. It's a way of saying, OK, I wasn't politically correct...but I'm not in the wrong really. There is also a racism embedded in many of the administrators who make appointments. A teacher of Indian extraction told me:

> I had an interview in a Catholic school, and when they debriefed me, all they could say was I used my hands too much when I talk...They were scared of telling me real reasons...Though most of the racism has come from outside school, my colleagues are respectful of my background – but I don't like to be told how well I speak English...

No doubt she can always hear the next word in the air: '...considering'.

Azizur Rahman is Muslim Community Leader in Ipswich, and goes into schools to talk about his religion. He takes a liberal line, tending more towards multiculturalism than anti-racism.

> I think this lady who doesn't want her daughter singing Pakistani songs will regret her decision in years to come, when her daughter goes to college and meets our people...We have to to learn to get on with each other. I'm opposed to single religion, single race schools, whether they're Jewish, Muslim, Christian, whatever they are...

Azizur Rahman has also stood out publicly in Ipswich against the Muslim Parliament. Like the advisory teacher, he felt that when children learned another language it was 'a gain, not a loss. I think learning another language is a good thing whatever the language is. Don't you?'

The Indian teacher said to me that, faced with parental anxiety about multicultural education, you need support 'from a whole school policy that everyone has discussed, and from the authority'. Perhaps as teachers we should go about reaching those objectives first. But a more pragmatic, and a thoroughly humane response, came from a white parent, who is also a secretary in a primary school. She said:

> I wouldn't mind my boy singing Pakistani songs, after all *they're* singing *our* songs. And I like them cooking foreign food, because I get to taste it.

Anyone who sees teachers as largely free of racism should read this frightening story in *Social Education and Personal Development* (Tattum and Tattum, 1992), taken from the Campaign for Racial Equality's report *Learning in Terror*, 1988:

> At a primary school...a black child was forced by the teacher to stand up and spell out the word 'golliwog' when the child refused to read it out in class because he found it offensive...

What follows are some examples of multicultural and anti-racist education in practice.

Paula Sorhaindo is a student reading for a BA degree in Independent Studies at Suffolk College, Ipswich. In her original plan for her degree course (these plans are designed by the students in consultation with tutors both inside and outside the college), she gives us a clear picture that reflects her 'personal experience' of what it is like to be a black person emigrating from her home country to England. ('There may,' she writes to me later, 'be black people who had an OK time.') Her subject is education as a means of combating racism:

> Racism was not an issue for me whilst growing up in Dominica...It wasn't until I came to England that I found my colour was a problem to some people...I also noticed that the children at my school were not taking education as seriously as we were brought up to do in Dominica...People only greeted you here [in England] if they knew you, but in Dominica we were told to acknowledge people in the streets even if you did not know them...I did not feel welcomed in England...Racism had hit me right in the face and I was powerless. No-one had warned my parents that they would suffer in this way. They were always seen as the MOTHER COUNTRY's children back home and now people acted as though they did not want them

around. Soon I started to blot Dominica from my life. The teachers were not interested in the knowledge I could have brought to the classroom...

Inspired by teachers, advisers and the work and example of Maya Angelou, Paula Sorhaindo began to work as a writer and performance poet.

In 1991 I got offered a job working for the multicultural adviser for Norfolk. I was assigned to teach poetry to High School children. The programme was to include History, Geography and various arts. I was also appointed to work with a junior school there...the first day of this job was a nightmare. Before I could even begin the lesson I was bombarded with names like PAKI, NIGGER, ZULU. The teacher was so embarrassed...

He wasn't going to let Paula work with these pupils, but Paula stood up to him:

I told him that these were the children I wanted to work with most of all...They had never seen a black person before except for on the TV and these images were often stereotyped...From this experience I realised it was part of my job to make sure that schools realise the need and importance of anti-racist education...

Paula Sorhaindo has written poems about her experience of racism. This is from 'Don't Colour Me Brown':

Colour me
an emotion
something lying inside
like stagnating tears
Colour me
a feeling
someone who doesn't fall
under hefty pride
Colour me
pain
that stays with me
slavery chains long
Colour me
a scent
that flows
like coconut oil
Colour me
a mood

that changes
Winter to Spring
Colour me
individual
Mahogony
Chestnut
Spice
there's so many shades
don't colour me brown
Colour me
Person

I watched Paula Sorhaindo teach in a Montessori nursery school near Woodbridge in Suffolk, in a house on the edge of this country town. As we arrived, the teacher, Melissa Stockdale, asked Paula if she'd seen a Montessori nursery before: 'It's very free...' It was much like some of the good local authority nurseries I've seen: displays of children's work, comfortable carpeted areas, an area where water stained with paint wouldn't matter when it hit the floor. Children all over the room were doing different things: painting, talking, playing, modelling.

Georgina, aged nearly 4, looked round as I approached. On the top of her easel was a painting, and on the top of that it said in adult printing: 'Georgina. A rainbow'. I pointed to an arc of paint at the top of her paper. 'So that's a rainbow. It's lovely,' I said. 'No,' said Georgina, pointing to another, lower, arc of colour. '*That's* the rainbow...' I asked her how old she was. 'Three'. I reflected in the car later that I wished all children had that courage to contradict an adult who is wrong. Perhaps giving them that courage, rather than teaching them that obedience is always right, except when there is a risk of abuse, is the way forward.

A parent said to me years ago, 'The trouble with you teachers is you are always teaching them to question everything ...' Here is the crux: should we teach obedience (mere training in the terms of this book) or should we educate? I have argued that not teaching children to question endangers them (chapter 4). In this pleasant place, with these privileged children, we can afford to get them to question. We can afford not to train them. Something tells us that their questioning, growing from material security, will not threaten us. Georgina begins at a point which many other children will never reach, and this underwrites her freedom to question, in the same way that poverty and unemployment underwrite oppression and violence.

On the wall of the Woodbridge nursery school was a piece of card, there purely for the staff's and (presumably) the parents' benefit, with the word Caribbean in the middle, and the words nature, science, biology, geography, drama, music, movement, maths, language, craft, cooking and visits at the end of lines radiating from it. There was also a list of duties for the day – giving out biscuits, tidying up – and the names of the children who had to fulfil them were fitted into little cuts in the card. There was also the ubiquitous Letterland alphabet, child head height, around part of the room.

The only immediate differences between this place and the nursery where my wife teaches in a working class school in Ipswich were in the names. Here were Fenella, Georgina, Johnathan, Isobel. There were Wayne, Sharon and Scott. Here was the grassy, very traditional English setting: a shiny wooden floor in a slightly cold large old house in perfect autumnal weather. In one corner was some mini furniture, a tiny *chaise-longue* and a sofa. On one wall was a display – and all the human figures in it were black, an unusual feature in any classroom, I'd say.

I often visit the nursery where my wife teaches. There, too, black, south Asian and Far Eastern faces are as frequent as white ones. On the 'How tall are you?' measure, on the weather chart, on the book covers, there are faces of all kinds. I find a half-completed jigsaw of a Sikh family sitting down for a meal, and as many black dolls in the Home Corner as there are white ones. There are labels in Gujerati, Bengali and Cantonese. The staff's names are given in Bengali or Syleti in the entrance hall. There are Chinese paperbacks on a table, and I am momentarily nonplussed by the fact that what should in my world be the front cover is at the back. There are Chinese recipes on a wall (it is new year) next to notices that announce:

READING WRITING AND SPELLING
A new group for women only with a crèche available

and

ASSERTIVENESS FOR WOMEN
These courses are being run by the local education authority.

At Woodbridge, Paula puts down on a table some Dominican objects. Then, after the children have gathered on the rug, she is introduced by Melissa: 'Paula has come from Dominica in the West Indies, so she knows much more about it than we do... ' Paula begins to tell the children about 'the necklace of islands in the Caribbean – each one is a pearl'.

Later, it emerges that the children know something already about the Caribbean, because it is part of Montessori practice to have a folder about each of the continents in the world. The African folder, for example, has photographs of young girls in head-dresses, children in a school, cities with cars tearing round huge roundabouts. Labels on these folders correspond to colours on globes and maps nearby. As Melissa says later, 'In infant schools they all seem to do topics on ourselves. "What about the world?" I always think.' A little more of the social is required, she believes – not in place of the personal, but because the personal can only be seen meaningfully in social terms. And that social is here, clearly, not just the milkmen and the doctors and the nurses – but the rest of the world that is very strange to us until someone like Paula comes in.

What Melissa is saying also attacks another notion about young children and learning. This is the prevalent idea that they can only learn about familiar, and therefore by implication, easy things, like shops and churches and local roads and our own bodies. On the contrary, she is saying in her practice, they are ready to deal with anthropology, geography. They are ready to learn about places that often do not concern their parents. What is there except me and the rest of the world? For Melissa Stockdale, the rest of the world is an exciting, distant place that people like Paula can bring closer, a place where we are all citizens.

So Paula isn't working unbroken ground. And I am learning something – that not all private schools celebrate the uni-racial; that some, although they are all white and uni-class, are ready to acknowledge what the world is really like. I'm not saying this is easy. I wish I could identify the demon in me that says this state of affairs is unfair. Is that demon some sort of liberal? It suggests, first, that it is glad these children are learning these lessons and, secondly, that the context is too comfy. That where the less comfortable children are, there are going to have to be fewer comfy lessons taught. That this is a beautiful multiculturalism that must have its counterpart elsewhere, something stronger, something aggressive, to stand up to the racists at the football ground, the British National Party in the Millwall ward in South London.

Paula shows the children at Woodbridge pictures in a folder – a Caribbean shop, a carnival with men dressed in scarlet as the devil, others dressed in black as witches, herself and her daughter dressed in traditional costume, the wobdwiett, local wildlife like agoutis, manikous, toads (*'crappeau,'* says Paula, with a glance at the staff). There are the interruptions you would expect: 'I want a wee' ('Go on then,' says Melissa).

Johnathan is the youngest, only three, a handsome little blond boy in corduroys and he laughs raucously and falsely at times: 'A-a-a-a-a-a-a-.' He moves his hands around, then flaps them in other children's faces, then observes that this is having no effect, because the other children (and the teachers) are intent on Paula; so he gives up disconsolately. Then he says, vaguely, not to anyone, in quick succession, 'Where's Kate? Kate isn't here today. Kate's gone on her holiday. I didn't go on a holiday...'

Another child interrupts, too, 'My mum's going to make me a pirate costume... ' and Paula accepts the interruption: 'And you're going to a carnival?' At times, it might seem to a visitor – an inspector, perhaps – to be a mayhem of 'I like, I hate, I want, I've got, I'm going to, I won't'. But each of these openings is an opening on to a central statement about our being human. When we say things like this in the staffroom, they are accepted as part of life: 'I can't stand the way that child looks at me, that look in his eyes...' I heard someone say in a middle school. Two teachers gave the speaker a look, but most of the rest of his colleagues seemed to accept this as a part of living. But we condemn the children's 'I like, I hate, I want, I've got, I'm going to, I won't' as a disorganised mess. It is simply the way we talk about how the rest of the world looks to us.

Then Paula puts down the file of pictures, and picks something up. 'This is a calabash'. They relish the word, saying it, not in unison, around the group: 'Ca-la-bash'. She compares it with a pumpkin, and after some open-ended questioning, shows them a mask made from a calabash. The children are impressed by this – they show it again by their sudden and total silence. Once again I am struck – for, it can't be, but it seems, the millionth time – by how we can control children through offering them first hand experiences. Suddenly the like, the hate, the want, the won't, are silenced.

But we can educate them thus as well. Because, with photographs, we are asking them, once again, to take our word (or picture) for things. With objects, on the other hand, we are offering them a primary source that they can criticise, that they can then claim as theirs, that they can despise, or praise.

Paula shows them a shakshak, and a wobdwiett, and again the children are silent, enchanted by the beautiful clothing and the promise that one of them might have a chance to wear it soon. There is a seedpod, and someone says it is a banana, and Paula pretends to eat it. Whatever it is, it is real, not a photograph, and the children believe because it is palpably there.

Then she says she will tell them a story. But before she can, Melissa (who went out of the room a moment ago) produces a plate with little pieces of pineapple. 'I thought we could have some pineapple, because they' (the children, not the pineapple pieces) 'have been sitting very still for quite a long time.' It is, in fact, about forty minutes, and I think they could do with a stretch or even a run around. Everyone has some, except Lena (the assistant) and me and some children who 'hate' pineapple.

Then Paula tells her story, about the first tree in the world. And this is magical. Paula's eye contact, her actions, her extrovert sound effects, all entrance the children. Meanwhile, I make my notes, and Melissa has her video camera going. One boy joins in. 'The berries –' says Paula. 'Poisonous!' says the boy. 'We're going to –' says Paula. 'Chop down the trees,' says the boy.

As Paula and the teachers go to get the area ready for the making of the first tree, Georgina, who is three, tells me she can hop, and shows me, to prove it, hopping round in a little circle.

Today I am in another, very differently situated nursery. The road outside is busy, being one of the main arteries taking traffic into and out of this large county town. Looking around at the children, I can see that at least a quarter of them are from ethnic minorities. The Asians, it turns out later, are from the large Bangladeshi community in the town. There are also one or two African Caribbean children.

You enter the nursery down a little corridor, squashing yourself against the wall to let two women with push chairs go past. On the walls are photographs of human beings: children, adults – but the most arresting feature of the display is that most of the figures are black or Asian. There is writing in several languages – not just the usual WELCOME/WILKOMMEN notice with Gujerati and

Bengali on it. One of these languages is Syleti, a language spoken in the Sylet area of Bangladesh where nearly all Bengalis in Britain come from. Indeed, something like eighty percent of all Indian restaurants in the UK are owned and staffed by Syletis.

I am here to watch the headteacher take an assembly on racism. Only the junior children are present. As we walk in, the record player is playing Billie Holiday's recording of 'Strange Fruit', a song about the lynching of black men in the Deep South by the Ku Klux Klan. Children's heads sway to the syncopated rhythm. As someone turns the volume down, the headteacher reads the words of the poem solemnly over the fading tenor sax. Then she says: 'Can you name some things which are almost completely of the twentieth century?...Of course, there are many.' A list comes from the children: Aeroplanes. Cars. Exhaust fumes. Machine guns. Computers. Plane crashes. Plastic. The hole in the ozone layer. Colour photography. Television.

> What other things can you think of? We could put them in two lists, good things and bad things. Of course some things are neither completely good nor completely bad. And you can't have cars, yet, without fumes. Or aeroplanes without crashes. Or [with a sly look at the staff sitting at the side of the hall] television without Australian soaps. There's one thing the twentieth century has produced that some people think is wholly good. And that is jazz.
>
> This music came originally out of the music played on plantations in the USA in the middle of the last century. The people who played were slaves, whose parents and grandparents had been brought from Africa in terrible ships across the Atlantic Ocean. Some of the music was descended from Christian hymns, and these songs expressed longing for a lost homeland.

Here she plays a snatch of 'Just a closer walk with thee'.

> Other songs were more secular, or worldly, in character. They were about love and pain, and simply being human. Many of the slaves who were herded into the ships died. We can imagine how the others suffered – from hunger, thirst, imprisonment, indignity – and, if they had time for it, boredom. Let's listen to this record ['Strange Fruit'] again. What instruments can you hear?

The children identify trumpet, saxophone, piano, guitar, bass, drums.

> If we listen carefully to this song, we find it is a poem set to music and we find it's a very strange and terrible piece of writing. The fruit

that hangs from the trees in the southern states of the USA isn't what you and I would call fruit at all. It isn't apples, or oranges, or berries.

It is the bodies of men, who have been murdered – lynched (lynched means murdered by lots of people, all running at the victim at the same time) – and hung from the trees. The black men who have been killed by the Ku Klux Klan. This was an organisation of white men in the south who persecuted black people because they believed in the supremacy of what they called 'the great white race'.

Someone called this song 'a grim song of death'. Another writer said that when she sang the song, 'you saw in Billie the wife or sister or mother of one of the victims beneath the tree... '

The children are silent. I reflect that some of the headteacher's words are difficult, but her way of talking – varied, paced – contributes to the effect she is having. Also, on one wall are LP covers depicting Louis Armstrong and Billie Holiday, and a poster for a long-gone jazz event at a nearby theatre. A pack of material about the slave trade is spread out on a table, with a copy of *Black History for Beginners* by Denise Dennis and Susan Willmarth. A class has written poems about being a slave. There is a large computer-printed legend over all this, a quotation from Martin Luther King:

NOW IS THE TIME TO MAKE JUSTICE A REALITY FOR ALL OF GOD'S CHILDREN

The headteacher continues:

Not all the discrimination against black people in the southern states of the USA was as tragic as this. In New York, Billie Holiday, the singer on that record, whom many consider to be the greatest ever jazz singer, was subjected to racial prejudice. She was touring with a white band, led by the clarinetist Artie Shaw. Artie, a Jew, was a white man. Billie told a reporter once:

[Here another teacher reads Billie Holiday's words from a popular biography]

'I was billed next to Artie himself, but was never allowed to visit the dining room, as did other members of the band. I had to enter and leave the hotel through the kitchen, and had to remain in a little dark room all evening until I was called on to do my numbers...'

The manager told Artie that southerners in the audience were complaining that she was using the passenger lift. 'She must go in the goods lift from now on,' he told Artie.

Artie said later, 'Her eyes glazed...she said later, "What a thing to happen in a hotel named after Abraham Lincoln..."' Abraham Lincoln was the president who had freed the slaves. Roy Eldridge, the great black trumpet player who joined Artie Shaw's band, was refused admission to a hall where he was supposed to be playing. He got in at last, and described later how he played his set: '...tears were rolling down my cheeks. I don't know how I made it. When you're on stage you're great, but as soon as you come off, you're nothing...'

Jazz didn't remain as the music of the black races. Many white men in America learned about its power, its strength in making us laugh, cry, think, feel.

When bands of white and black players were touring in the southern states, the white players could stay in any hotel they wanted. The black players, however, had to stay in hotels reserved for them, and these places were not usually very pleasant.

Someone once said that Billie Holiday suffered from an incurable disease – being born black in a white society.

We live in a society that can contain everyone. That is, if we look for the riches that each of us owns. That is our purpose today: to celebrate our differences and our common humanity. Can any of you tell me how someone has put you down because of something about you?

At first the answers are about red hair, freckles ('my dad always laughs about my freckles'...'Do you mind that?'...'Yes I do ...'), but eventually a Sikh boy says, 'At _____ [the local high school] you get detention more if you are Asian, or if you are black'. There are murmurs of assent to this from all around the hall, and the headteacher collects some of them. Then she says

Today and for the rest of this week we are going to put complaints about times when people are unfair to us in a box, and we are going to talk about them in our classes...

Eventually Billie Holiday's voice emerges again, and the children file out, some still swaying slightly. I can only speculate on their learning. Perhaps they are reflecting on the obvious passion their headteacher has for jazz; on her evident sincerity about justice for all people. Perhaps they are thinking about some of the remarks children have made in answer to the headteacher's question about unfairness in the school, and maybe even linking those remarks to the Luther King quotation, which you simply can't miss: JUSTICE. REALITY. GOD'S CHILDREN. Perhaps they are imagining themselves on a slave ship, or in chains, or looking at the 'strange fruit hanging from the poplar trees'.

Three eight year old girls are planning a poem. They have in front of them an old Open University Unit *The Yorubas of Nigeria* from the original Humanities Foundation Course (1970); an original painting by the Yoruba artist, Emmanuel Jegede; and photographs of Yoruba artefacts from the local museum. I have told them about the weakling child who dies in the first week, who is, in Yoruba mythology, called 'Abiku', and who is regarded as a fierce spirit seeking to return to the wild. They are reading Wole Soyinka's poem 'Abiku' (printed in the OU unit, in Soyinka's collection *Idanre* and in other places).

I leave the girls for some twenty minutes, and when I return they have produced the first draft of their poem. Once again, it seems to me that the arts can give us insights into other ways of looking at the world. We noticed this, for example, with the children writing about death in chapter 2, and with the poems about housework in chapter 5. Regrettably, the first draft of the girls' poem is lost. What follows was a third draft made after some heated group conversation, and after corrections of spelling and syntax by me:

Abiku

I am going back to the darkness.
I am going to the inside of the earth.
I am going to crusty, dry inside.
Nothing will stop me.

I don't want to bother
with all the work.
I want to go back
to the inside of the earth.

I am going back.
I don't want to see the sun,
I don't want to see the moon,
I don't want to see the grass or trees.

I am going back
where I don't have to be bothered with the light.
I want to be like a bird
that's burnt in its egg.

I am like a flower
that has not opened out.
My petals are all closed up.
The earth is too noisy for me.

I am not staying in this light, bright world.

I want to go back to the wildness
where it is all dark and crackling,
it is all dry and wrinkled.

I want to drift down the river
to where I can rest.

No-one can change my plans.

The children are learning to empathise with another race by looking at a haunting example of its poetry. They are learning about form – they have taken Soyinka's and adapted his rhythms half consciously to make new ones. They are learning about poetry – 'I want to be like a bird/that's burnt in its egg' is a beautiful version of Soyinka's line 'the snail is burnt in his shell'. They are learning to collaborate. Above all they are learning that it is not only illegal to be racist in the classroom – it also gets in the way of our being fully human, of understanding what all of us must learn: that, in our potential, we are more than Jew or Greek, black or white, Asian or African, male or female.

This chapter has looked at the distinction between multicultural and anti-racist education. Little of either happens in our schools, still. My bias here to the gentler multicultural approach is the result of what practice I have been able to observe. And however gentle it may be, the multicultural option is still very powerful education. To open up the rest of the world; to show off the resources other races have; to discuss democratically practices and beliefs different from our own – this can only enrich our curriculum by giving children choices to help them answer for themselves the fundamental question: How shall I live?

My final note is a warning: if the National Curriculum drifts back towards kings-and-queens history, and away from what happened to the ordinary people – for example, on the plantations and in the slave ships – it will further institutionalise racism, and back up the British National Party; it will build for the children we teach a society where only some of them will be fulfilled, and the rest will be alienated. And the alienated children will have been seriously harmed, and they will be justifiably angry.

CHAPTER SEVEN

Stories: talking about PSME

Learning happens through stories. Not just the stories we tell, not even chiefly those; but in the stories they tell us. In the stories they live and we live; in the stories we see everyday in the classrooms, to which we are tempted to give neat punchlines, but which are really as untidy and real and scrappy as life itself. And as gripping. And as disturbing. That will sometimes make our readers say, or write in our margins: 'This is grisly, I don't want to know any more about this'. And as funny, and, every so often, as glorious...

> From an anonymous teacher's classroom journal

I need to explore and make
something, however little,
and break it off from myself
in the power of my spirit.

The most important word in the title of this book is 'education'. To appreciate this, we need only reflect what impression I would have given had I replaced 'education' with 'training'. Education has the function of *increasing*, while training has the function of *decreasing* the possibilities that emerge when we play with our environment. Education explores, training determines. The entry for 'education' in the 1824 edition of *Encyclopaedia Britannica* said (in an entry written by James Mill, the father of John Stuart Mill) that

The end of education is to render the individual...an instrument of happiness, first to himself and next to other beings...Education... denotes the means which may be employed to render the *mind*, [his italics] as far as possible, an operative cause for happiness...

> (*An anthology of pieces from the early editions of Encyclopaedia Britannica*, 1963)

These lovely sentences *increase* possibilities. It is odd that the 15th edition of *Britannica* opens its massive entry on Education with an altogether more reactionary, more mechanistic, more *decreasing* note than the one sounded by Mill senior: 'education can be thought of as the transmission of the values and accumulated knowledge of a society'. This perspective leads to a hefty emphasis on obedience – see chapter 4 for comments on the problems this presents for teaching children to say 'No' when their sexual autonomy is threatened – and acceptance of current values, which may suit those with power, but which may not suit the rest of us. This view locks children in the chains of the past.

Indeed, there can simply be no handing down, no 'transmission of values' that is merely that in a non-problematical way, because the act of handing down, or of seeing the handing down as non-problematical, must be a value statement. Common sense in education ('obviously children need to know the kings and queens of England...') as in everything else is a conservative value position, because it conserves values rather than questions them. Much of its power derives from the fact that it is not perceived as a value position at all (conservative or otherwise). If we see PSME as a non-problematical transmission of facts and skills about, for example, travel competence or smoking or keeping fit, we are denying its force and power, and merely being advisers; we are reacting impotently to society's current panics. If we insist on the importance of the history of kings and queens, we are making unspoken – yet potent – statements about the importance of the history of the common people.

Common sense is a weak notion for anyone concerned with education, and this can be demonstrated by a list of statements. It was once common sense

- to punish lack of effort in a child by placing him or her in a corner wearing a dunce cap
- to teach boys woodwork and girls needlework
- to make children Christians by preaching about hellfire (see, for example, the sermon in Joyce's *Portrait of the Artist as a Young Man*).

We might in groups as teachers develop sets of practices that seem like common sense now, but which will look as absurd and cruel as these former commonsensical statements look now. One might be, for example, that the availability of violin lessons should depend on parents' ability and readiness to pay. Another might be about the common practice that children who have difficulty learning to read should have *more* one-to-one torture exploring the areas of failure, while children who have problems with music or games should have *less* practice at these subjects. How will this look in a hundred years time?

Looking at Mill's claims for education, I reflect that there is a certain unpredictability about happiness: its operative causes are never certain. That is why education, which deals with all the increasing unpredictability that being human implies, and training, which attempts to deal in certainties that decrease our options, differ so radically. That is why, in educational settings, we must be constantly alert for common sense's sleight of mind and its merely contemporary, usually vocational, applications.

And working class children can play the violin. Dunce caps don't work, except to make dunces. There is no good reason why boys and girls should not have the same curriculum. We do not improve practice by concentrating on little bits where we fail, but by developing enthusiasm for the whole.

There are many ways thought systems suggest we are determined or forced into certain tracks. To a Marxist, we are determined by our social class; to a Calvinist, by God 'before the world began'; to an evangelical Christian, we are determined by original sin as wiped away by grace; to a Freudian, we are determined by our unconscious and by our deep, secret relations with our parents. Behaviourist psychology has, arguably, the most rigid determining structure, insisting that every act is determined by stimuli outside our control. It is against all this that education stands as a potentially freeing agent, as an instrument 'of happiness' as Mill puts it, and it is not fanciful to identify the various determinisms as elements in training. All of them are open to human abuse that strengthens even more their controlling possibilities, as a political, religious or psychological system is used for the benefit of the power of a hegemonic group.

A letter writer to *The Independent*, during a controversy about Religious Education in schools, wrote that 'it is not possible to be taught that there is a God, only to be told it'. It is the very ineluctability of, for example, behaviourist concepts that makes the educational struggle against them and away from them so vital. It is encouraging to educationists that there are so many determinist systems. After all, they can't all be right.

The de-educationalised classroom

While it might seem like stating the obvious to say that schools, like this book, are primarily concerned with education, there are classrooms in which strategies have been developed over years which relegate learning to a position below administrative convenience, and reduce schools to a position even lower than training establishments. A school can be personal, social and moral – and not educational. Indeed, a school cannot but be at positions or points on continua which have at each end of them, respectively, personal/impersonal, social/nonsocial, and moral/amoral. (I use 'amoral' in a sense that suggests that a school is not concerned with morality, only with learning in a traditionally conceived academic sense. A politician once told me that schools should realise they are about learning facts, not about 'making the world a better place and getting on together'). All schools have a standpoint on these issues. But while all schools have the same standpoint on education – they all believe in their educational efficacy – some schools are hardly educational at all, and all schools have many moments in their lives when acts happen that are not education. Some of these are necessary. We have to take the register, in case there is a fire. We have to collect money for school trips. We have, in a sense, to police our schools so that they are safe places. But other acts happen that are not so necessary. This story comes from the south-west of England. I have fictionalised all the names.

The Story of Roland

'Shut up' says Roland suddenly, in the quiet classroom. It's full of ten-year-old children about to settle down to a poetry session from a visiting writer, me. Roland is speaking to a boy near his desk. 'Shut up shouting across my classroom'. He holds eye contact with the boy for a long time – ten seconds or so – and the boy looks back at him, nervously.

This reminds me of a parent talking to the headteacher Liz Waterland in Waterland's *Not a Perfect Offering*:

> One teacher, he had a pneumatic finger we called it. Drove it straight into your chest so you had to walk backwards to the wall and then he had you. DON'T. YOU. EVER. DO. THAT. AGAIN...

Eye contact and ten seconds and finger and the word 'my' all represent an imperialist violence that says this is my place, not yours. I make a note. I will ask Roland whether I can use his classroom in my book, but not yet. Just for now I'll take the precaution of not using his real name. In any case, he isn't here as a villain, but as a representative of the teacher in all of us who is more concerned about his or her own power than about the children's autonomy. Perhaps I'll ask him to comment on my story, to put his side...In the meantime, I go on listening and writing while Roland directs his class. 'Table 1 – shoes in rack. Table 2 – shoes in rack. Table 1 – milk. Table 3 – shoes in rack. Table 2 – milk...' He talks like a timetable, or an old fashioned speak-your-weight machine, clipped, robotic, verbless. There are no ambiguities, no chances of misunderstanding him.

Before the children start to write, I quote to them, from where I stand at the back of the classroom, a boy in another class who has written half an hour ago, 'The cat laps milk, lap after lap, like a racing driver'. The children look at me, and some laugh. 'Very good,' says a boy in front of me appreciatively, unironically. He nods. Then other children get the joke. Roland sits at his desk at the front of the room, checking lists of names, ignoring this conversation. But the boy's pun is, to me, evidence of agile, witty thinking, the kind of behaviour we ought, as educators, to encourage. Later, another child shows that he has picked up the idea of the pun, as he writes the first line of his riddle 'The Lion': 'His head is mainly gold...' Warming to the theme, another child writes a Christmas riddle that contains the line 'at the present time'.

What has made Roland so utterly indifferent to success like this? Who has taken away from him the joy of appreciating a pun? How has his obsession with order so effectively demolished his sense of fun? One factor in his negative behaviour is me. If his behaviour is imperialist in its controlling techniques, what is mine? I have been imposed on his territory like a missionary. Who do I think I am? Well, I think I am a teacher/writer with water to sprinkle on the poems these children have inside them, but from Roland's point of view I am...what? A distraction from the real purpose of schooling, the delivery of the National Curriculum? A cocky rival who controls his class in less obvious ways than he does?

When Jack, who is sitting near Roland, starts to write, Roland helps him by sounding out phonics like a first year drama student asked to play someone speaking to a deaf person who is beginning to learn to lip-read. Later he says to me, 'Jack can't write', so, contrarily, I make a point of praising Jack's fractured, ill-spelt but nevertheless original effort, which is about a room full of ghosts:

The bald ones are ghosts
and the hairy ones
are dead bodies
The bald ones are ghosts
and the hairy ones
are dead bodies.

Later Jack said to me, 'The bald ones are ghosts and the hairy ones are dead babies,' and I copied that down, and then he in turn copied it. There is a drawing of ten ghosts lying in a bed. 'Sere' is 'square'. 'Gosthe' is obviously 'ghosts'. Jack has come up with little bits of school lore largely unrelated to the stimulus: 'Ten in the bed and the little one said...'; and there is a strong hint of reading scheme in 'The room is square. It is a square room'.

Roland goes off to do something or other about a new disciplinary problem ('The infants have been rampaging in the flower beds, and we want decent roses next year') and I send Jack on an errand. This is to reward him for his efforts. He never gets the little perks, like four or five minutes walking free round the school that meant so much to me when I was 10. 'Can you ask Mrs Banham for some notepaper?' He is pleased to be asked, and goes off. Then Roland comes in with the boy behind him: 'Fred, Jack gets a bit confused...was it notepaper or newspaper?' I take this as a rebuke for sending Jack off at all. In fact, it emerged he had understood me. I wonder how I'd feel if someone said about me, as no doubt they will, one day, 'Fred gets a bit confused sometimes'. Then Jack reads his writing to the class, and as he starts, Roland says to the girl standing next to him, loudly enough for me to hear at the back of the room, 'Help him out, Frances, when he gets stuck'.

Who has persuaded Roland that Jack can be treated so disrespectfully? What does he think is happening in Jack's spirit when he hears this? Or in Frances' spirit?

In the hall, there is trouble. 'You will end up in jail, young man,' a male teacher's voice says. A boy is being confronted by Roland and another teacher. He has been fighting. 'He goes for the eyes, for the throat, he's like an animal when he gets going,' says Roland to me, miming the actions. Now he stands glaring at the boy and I try to get through the hall without being noticed, but at the same time noticing everything myself.

Another day when I arrive at the school at eight-thirty in the morning, Roland has just come down from the roof. He is wearing overalls, and has been painting guttering with the sort of paint that marks clothes indelibly, and which therefore deters potential breakers-in. He rubs his hands together in theatrical pleasure at the discomfiture of anyone unwise enough to try anything on now. On another occasion I take an assembly. I read, with children taking part, a long poem about the creation; then children read their poems; then I quote a bowdlerised version of Dylan Thomas's remark about why he wrote poetry: 'I write poetry for glory of God and the pleasure of man – and I'd be a damn fool if I didn't'. The bowdlerisation is there to avoid the swearing and what we would now call sexist language. The children sit throughout in silence. Afterwards, Roland thanks me and says to the children, 'Well done, you sat very still – *most* of you...'

There is little education in any of this. There is discipline, and discipline that is constantly on the watch for bad behaviour – expecting it in fact. There is a great concern for order – Roland is like W. B. Yeats in his Fascist phase in one respect. 'In politics,' Yeats wrote, 'I have but one passion and one thought, rancour against all who, except under the most dire necessity, disturb public order...' Roland is constantly marching through the school keeping order, and where the need for order and the need for learning clash, there is no doubt which will win. Jean, an infant teacher in Waterland's book, 'never felt settled with a class until she'd had her first row with them'. By contrast, Roland never has rows: he is in a constant occupying war of attrition, attempting to subdue the natives; rewarding the compliant ones with little privileges, and keeping down any potential rebels . There is also administration in Roland's game, and training in phonics. There is a concern for security. This security extends to the point where Roland protects the classroom as his.

Teachers who, unlike Roland, are interested in educational moments, sometimes complain that current demands on their time cause them to neglect these moments, and also to neglect their private lives. Any teacher's partner will confirm this, seeing another Sunday afternoon drowned in a flood of checklists and other administrative trivia. This de-educationalisation has links to the government legislation referred to in the Introduction. Doctors are complaining as I write the first draft of this (June 1993) that changes in the NHS have increased their administrative workload. According to an article in *The Independent on Sunday* (27 June 1993) broadcasters at the BBC are 'drowning in paper' because of 'Producer Choice'. 'Even borrowing a book from the BBC library has to be costed nowadays'. The police, too, are complaining, about 'excessive paperwork'. The substantive issues of our professions – education, patient care, broadcasting, policing – have been removed, and replaced with what Causley, in his poem 'School at Four o'clock' (*Collected Poems*, 1975) calls 'useless bits of paper'. This makes Roland's emphases under-standable.

What else led Ronald to behave like this? How is it that all of us have elements of this sort of behaviour at some points in our teaching? We learn to be controlling and irascible partly from our own teachers. I asked a newly qualified teacher what first drew her to teaching, and with remarkable frankness she replied that she'd envied her teachers' power when they wrote 7/10 on her writing. I remember the awe with which I watched Mr Davies, our French teacher, lose – or pretend to lose – his temper, and how he could silence a form room of rough third-year grammar school boys with a glare. If I push myself, I can recall the sense of power I felt, alongside the delight, in my first classroom as a young teacher. The point about Roland is not to vilify him, but to see in our practice as teachers the obsession with power, the will to control; and also to see what learning is, and then to increase the learning day by day, and decrease the control.

The question for the teachers who stand for the PSME element in schools' lives is, how do we re-educate ourselves and the children? How can we draw ourselves away from the negative certainties that administration and discipline (as traditionally conceived) provide for us, and learn to live with uncertainties and doubt? That is what staff development in this area has to deal with, and it is a tall order, because at every point in INSET sessions these days someone will try to wrest the process away from learning, from education, to elements of a programme that is administrative/political, and not educational. And, of course, in this way, the government's programme resembles Roland's.

Critically, the way we develop our practice in this area is PSME itself: there is no success possible in work imposed on staff, when the whole aim is greater autonomy for the children. Non-autonomous teachers will not teach children to be autonomous. Also, every moment of discussion about every detail is a point of entry into a way of looking at how children learn, and a way, by extension, of considering what we are as human beings. Thus we are taking on serious responsibilities as we question what learning is.

To stimulate more talk is not to suggest that we aren't, as they say, 'doing it' already. We are. We are doing PSME in our arrangements for looking after sick children – do they have privacy, or do they have to sit on chairs outside the secretary's room? Mr

Gradgrind was doing PSME when he preached the centrality of the fact, as opposed to the importance of feeling and intuitive knowledge. He wouldn't, of course, have been able to acknowledge that, much as politicians are unable to admit the existence of their own politics when they accuse opponents of being 'politically motivated'. Roland is teaching his children volumes of curriculum that is PSME. He is, for example, teaching them that his authority is not to be questioned; that certain members of his class are more valued than others; that a school runs essentially on administrative detail. It was in his school that I found Michele's Elliott's book *Feeling Happy Feeling Safe: A Safety Guide for Young Children* which has strategies for teaching children to say no. But in a classroom as obedience-obsessed as Roland's, it is plain daft to suddenly pop up with the importance of refusal in threatening situations. Saying no here is all too dangerous, like standing up to a mini-Stalin.

Nevertheless, we would be well advised to base our future theory on PSME on our current practice. I would like to bring to muzzy theory the precision of practice. In their book *Social Education and Personal Development* (1992) Delwyn and Eva Tattum say, 'practice must be grounded in theory'. I believe that this is the wrong way round, because practice always predates theory. Thus the model for development in PSME isn't reading books and seeing what we must do next, but seeing what we are doing now, the collaborative review and criticism of it, and the development of a theory that will take us forward. It is also the search for what is missing, for what isn't happening. This is PSME for teachers.

Politics and PSME are there, like the air we breathe, in the classroom, and they are there in the meeting of teachers' minds. They are there in what is known, as neutrally as sleight of voice will allow, as the management of education. Some teachers claim, usually through frustration with both the established political order and their relations at work, that they have dropped politics, 'become apolitical'. Inevitably, though, it is the role of educated people to criticise the established order, just as it is the role of the established order to establish itself. Both theory and practice in education are about nothing more or less than the way lives are lived (or, as I mis-typed there, loved).

What can the stories in this book teach us about the way we might improve our work with children? Cavell and Holdbrook both teach us that 'in the beginning was the word' and that the word is in the centre with us now as we teach children. Schools are full of voices, and the more those voices are the voices of children, the more successful our work as teachers will be. Among all the impedimenta of the school's relationship with authority – ring folder upon ring folder – 'words are all we have', and to what extent are we leaving space for the children's words? How much are we able to set the children free to work out their own problems? Or do we lock them in a graveyard silence? Those schools, and Kexborough, teach us as well about the importance of openness in all areas of the curriculum, especially in the difficult ones like sex education and multiculturalism. In our staff development, how open are we to the words of all the teachers working in our schools?

A cautionary tale

The university lecturer has arrived. 'He has a little Fiat, hasn't he?...yes it's him'. The buzz goes round the staffroom and the admin area of the primary school. When he arrives – the only male in the staffroom, thirty-something – he impresses nearly everyone with his smile and his style.

The staff have decided to devote this term's curriculum meetings to their work on PSE, and Michael has a research interest in this area. At first, he asks them, 'What have you done so far?' The teachers talk about improvements they've made in playground provision – building climbing frames with the help of parents; developing a small adventure playground; making sure that the children have been consulted at all points on this development of their play area. They have designed and partly implemented policies on equal opportunities and combating racism. They talk, too, about the school rules, which were initially drafted by the children, through the medium of the now long-standing school's council; they feel that the school's style is what one teacher calls 'PSE-friendly', and many elements in their school are raised. Anyone familiar with the Plowden Report would recognise them: parents play a prominent part in the school; classroom organisation encourages child-talk. Throughout all this, Michael nods and nods and occasionally smiles.

A disagreement on the staff emerges. It concerns the way teachers should deal with what they see as anti-PSE elements in the National Curriculum. One teacher suggests that they could take a more confrontational stance: 'I'm getting to the point where I'm going to refuse to do things that are against my conscience. I've gone through all this depression bit...I think it's still all up for grabs, I really do...I don't think we should've kowtowed so easily...' Her colleague, Steph, murmurs quietly, 'It is the law, Sharon...'

Sharon glares. 'I know that, but...' Suddenly Michael leans forward with a glance at the headteacher, who is looking alternately at her two colleagues. 'Have you seen Smith and Weston's article on this?' he asks. 'They suggest...'

Suddenly the atmosphere is changed. The teachers were working towards a disagreement, possibly a noisy and dangerous one. Both of them recognised, with varying degrees of certainty, that this had to happen before any resolution: there is no resurrection without a crucifixion. To put it less dramatically, you've got to break the ground before anything can grow. They were taking the problem on. They were theorising with their children in mind, and their practice. But now this question about an article descends on the group.

Silence. Then, 'Er, no...' (Sharon). Michael says, 'It's a nice study...a nice study...They say...' And he tells them what they say. It's about innovation and ownership of data and about how teachers in some school have developed their PSE; how they related it to the National Curriculum, working out strategies for developing skills in dealing with management situations (etc. etc. etc...)

He has contaminated the setting with academic language, management jargon and a perceived expertise about theory as traditionally seen. The teachers' minds are taken off their own problem and its possible solutions, and tuned into an academic and managerial perspective. Some of the interference is a result of memories of their own tutors at college, however many years ago; some of it comes from a teacher's generic mistrust of theory. One or two of the teachers are visibly relieved at this development. Perhaps they were worried about a confrontation; but others regret a missed opportunity as the conversation floats away into anecdote about how other researchers have seen this problem dealt with in Australia, or Coventry, or somewhere – but not here.

There is, as I have hinted above, a considerable animus against theory in staffrooms, and this has led to ugly alliances between central government plans for initial teacher-education being centred solely on schools, and experienced teachers who remember being bored at college twenty years ago by Piaget. But it may well be that the fault isn't in the theory; that theory and practice are not, indeed, two ends of a continuum; but that our theories need to be developed in groups of teachers with coherent aims, and based on their practice. And also that we inevitably bring our personal lives to every professional setting. For a discussion on how the personal is always with us in our development as teachers, see Mary Jane Drummond's article 'Learning about gender in primary schools' in *Thinking about PSE in the Primary School*, edited by Peter Lang.

So I have two themes: openness, and the centrality of the word. But another one has been knocking on the door as I've been writing, and it will become explicit in my final pages.

Afterword

We must love one another or die

W H Auden, 'September 1939'

Humiliated (as he saw it) by the September 1938 Munich agreement between Chamberlain and Hitler, T. S. Eliot wrote in *The Idea of a Christian Society* (1939):

> We could not match conviction with conviction, we had no ideas with which we could either meet or oppose the ideas opposed to us. Was our society...assembled around anything more permanent than a *congeries* of banks, insurance companies and industries, and had it any beliefs more essential than a belief in compound interest and the maintenance of dividends?

Firstly, replace the obscure '*congeries*' with 'heap...pile...a collection of things merely heaped together' (*Shorter Oxford English Dictionary*). Secondly, change 'compound interest and the maintenance of dividends' to 'profit motive and the maintenance of growth'. Then we can see how neatly Eliot's comments suit the early 1990s, another decade when the British seem to be motivated, financially and educationally (and probably in other ways beyond the scope of this book), by a pile of unrelated objectives, rather than any central moral aim. We live in a winter of the moral imagination, comparable to the one Eliot lived in before the last World War. This is the social context in which we have to set our educational thinking, in which this book is written, in which we try to teach and learn.

In responding to her current political context, a teacher I know is fond of saying that Margaret Thatcher 'drove her back to God'.

What she means, I take it, is that there must be more moral, more *just*, values than those held by the governments that ruled in Britain from 1979. And for her, as for Eliot, these values live again in Christianity. This is partly because Christianity, through the metaphor of the money-changer in the temple, criticises powerfully the worshippers of 'the discipline of the marketplace'. Christianity insists, like other religions, on the value of the word, and how the word makes us human. And it also says, rather bluntly, through the mouth of St. Paul, that the love of money is the root of all evil.

But a return to what a fashionable and sentimental vision sees as a past of national religious observance will not lead to morally-based behaviour. On the contrary, John White (in *Education and the Good Life*) makes a powerful case for the contrary view when he criticises conservative thinking that states that questions of right and wrong are simple matters, soluble by reference to God and what He tells us, or by a national renewal based on a hoisting of the union flag over our schools. There are enough countries verging on theocracy to warn us against such thinking, and enough nationalist fundamentalisms to populate a hundred pure and horrible worlds. And we should carefully note ugly signs of a drift towards a one-religion state in circulars from the DFE that tell schools that they need a daily act of collective worship which is of 'a broadly Christian character'.

Behind the officialese and zenophobia of recent DFE publications is a desire for a curriculum that reflects more closely the values of a hegemonic group, the post-Thatcherite government ministers who talk about respect, only to mean respect for themselves and their institutions and values; who demonstrate almost daily, in real terms (that is, in terms of resources) their contempt for the old, the sick, and the poor.

It is not only religious people who have atavistic yearnings. In *Classroom Pedagogy and Primary Practice*, David McNamara assures us that it is the duty of teachers 'to communicate knowledge to others', as though knowledge constructed in the past, without necessary reference to the present, let alone its cutting edge into the future, is all we must recognize. Indeed, this view of knowledge sees children as able to bring nothing into school of any value compared to what the teacher, representing a nostalgic power, can offer: imperialistic history, for example, and a view of Shakespeare as the Bard who has nothing to ask of our times.

But, while conventional interpretations of religion give us problems, more imaginative approaches would help us to rediscover a source of values that exposes the emptiness of a community life based merely on money and the love of it. We must dig into the religious beliefs of all the communities in our society, and also into the humanism we can see in a thousand staffrooms, crossing all sorts of political boundaries. This humanism values what people say and do. It means understanding *who* we are, rather than *what* we are when placed on lists detailing our measurable achievements. Simone Weil puts this point beautifully when she tells us, 'To love one's neighbour is a question of being able to ask simply: What is your torment? Of knowing that affliction exists, *not as a statistic* (my italics)...but as something which happens to a human being...' Statistics are a part of the *congeries* that dominates our thinking, in the place where coherent public moral values should stand.

We also need a way of thinking about our humanity that sees ourselves as active learners, as participants with power of some sort in social settings, including schools. Then we can either let this power lie inert, or use it to help shape the world for the better. In contrast, we note the way in which OFSTED inspectors are being trained (here that verb *is* the correct one):

> The first afternoon we were given a case study of a school. The documentation was about the size of four telephone directories. But it was completely disorganized, not in alphabetic order as a phone book is... We were told to write a pre-inspection commentary on the school and identify key issues for inspections. We had two and a half hours for this, and we had to do it individually, there was no collaborative work...It was to be handed in at 6.30 the same day and if it was one minute late then that was recorded...
>
> We had to prepare an inspection timetable by 9.00 the next morning on the dot...I sat up till two because it was disorganized – schools are rich messy places where learning doesn't fit into neat little slots on the timetable. And then I didn't sleep...It went round and round in my head, I was obsessed, maybe I'd failed already, all my confidence had gone, I was drained, I couldn't think of anything else. People were crying, some people couldn't cope at all and went home...we were tested to destruction...It was the worst week of my professional life. People broke out in rashes, someone, a senior adviser somewhere, had heart palpitations for the first time in her life...

> (anonymous informant)

Here we have a dominant view of education as a deliverable mass of facts, thrown at the recipient with all the power of a bully. Human beings are reduced to tears and illness, and there is no room in my informant's head for anything except the mass of material pitched at him. He is not required to bring to the setting anything of himself; he is merely to obey his trainers, and to fulfil the gigantic tasks they have set him, tasks designed to disempower him. My informant continued:

> There were no green spaces, no time for reflection or conviviality... The only encouraging aspect of it all was that by Friday lunchtime, when we left, the groups had found a kind of *esprit de corps*, and I heard colleagues singing, to the tune of 'Guantanamera', 'One effin' OFSTED, there's only one effin' OFSTED...'

In my research for this book, I looked for staff in primary schools who could speak about convictions which informed their relationships with children; who could make explicit in one way or another, to some extent (note how these phrases push away my nervous coming to the point – we are all scared of this), a moral position. I asked for one-liners, mottos we might place over the front doors of our schools. My first contact, a first school head-teacher I'd known for twelve years, offered:

> *Each child is valued as an individual with rights and challenged as an individual with rights*

A teacher with whom I'd worked when he was both a student and a probationer said:

> *It's all about a relationship between teachers and children that is based on empathy and trust. Everything else – organisation, management, being state-of-the-art teaching-wise – is frills*

Another teacher in a junior school claimed the following as a collaborative aim:

> *We must empower children to become independent, confident people, both as learners and in relationships*

The same teacher offered this as her view:

> *For me it's about* agape, *practical compassionate love...*

A primary headteacher said:

> *It's about encouraging children to explore and enjoy and do the things they want without impinging on others*

I worried about this one, and couldn't see why, until I realised that most of what I enjoyed doing impinged almost entirely on others, whether that impinging involved the direct contacts of love and pain, or the reading and writing of words that might offend. Perhaps, I reflected, that is what it is to be a human being: one impinges on others.

Of course it depends on what you mean by 'individual', 'rights', 'empathy', 'independent', 'love'...Let's (as they used to say) 'unpack' these terms a little. How are teachers 'empathetic', 'loving', 'compassionate'? What does a 'confident', 'independent', 'learning' child look like? All these remarks are wearing their best clothes, and, as usual, best clothes are hiding something.

What emerges from this collection of comments is, first of all, an ideology with individuality at its centre. The first school head-teacher said that, while 'we were concerned in the past about individual children, now children are being reduced to a hypothetical child who has to attain this and that'. He might have gone further. The hypothetical children in the National Curriculum are not children as they are now, but always children as they will be. The National Curriculum ignores the process through which a child is moving, and concentrates on the hypothetical objective a child will reach. This places the weight, not on the child and her grasp of what life and learning is, but on what someone older thinks is going to be right for her (and all other children).

Despite the rhetoric of individualism, children are treated in large batches. Watch them as they queue up to go into assembly; as they are told when and where and even how to sit; note that what they wear is, more often than not, dictated to them by the very teachers who will then talk about treating them as 'individuals'. Again, expressions of individual characteristics – decorations on notebooks, hairstyles, pencil cases, badges – are constantly monitored and often discouraged as children are treated (in Louis MacNeice's phrases) like 'cogs in a machine' with their 'entirety' dissipated, their 'humanity' frozen. ('Prayer before birth', *Collected Poems*).

The second element in the teachers' ideology as expressed in these comments (especially the remarks about empathy) is an emphasis on human qualities, like trust, which are opposed to mechanistic ones. But although many teachers are empathetic and trusting, all too often the pressure on them in terms of work load shoves them into less kind, less respectful, treatment of children.

Thirdly, one teacher came up with the notion of empowerment. This is similar to the aim that John White says should have informed the National Curriculum from the beginning: personal autonomy. It was the last primary headteacher who presented the problem about autonomy: it's about encouraging children to 'explore and enjoy and do the things they want without impinging on others'. But many schools act as if their aims were to restrict children, to deny their autonomy. As a Board of Education 1909 Special Report, quoted by Alec Clegg and Barbara Megson in their 1968 book, *Children in Distress*, says

> Some schools exist in order to give so far as may be every child an equal chance of 'rising in the world'. Other schools exist to 'keep people in their place'.

And while this is still true, it is also true that all schools at some time exist to 'keep people in their place'. It is the task of the teacher of PSME to minimise these occasions, and to ensure that more often the school acts to help children 'rise in the world'. Clegg and Megson say that, by contrast, whenever a line is drawn at an exam point, or where testing happens, 'we tend to look above the line and admire, and the endeavours of those below the line are undervalued'.

In the end there is love. And I will define love as Simone Weil does, as 'the spirit of justice and truth that is nothing else but a certain kind of attention...' Love insists on what children call fairness, and what adults call justice; it is made real in the constant attention to what is happening under whatever surfaces we have laid down to hide reality. Love is research into the relationships between me, other people and the world, which aims at making the world a slightly fairer place at the end of each day. Love bids me welcome.

What is common to all these entities is risk, while, by contrast, the target structure of the National Curriculum is essentially a risk-reducing exercise. But empowering children involves risk above all else. Who knows, after all, what they might do next? My friends' two-year-old niece has just announced to the extended family that she has put her tongue into three-month-old James' mouth to see what it felt like. Children live in a world of play and experiment that is at once innocent and dangerous. But as James' father, a teacher, said to me, it's very rare you hear someone saying these days, 'Let's try it and see what happens'.

Love, above all, is a risk. C. S. Lewis says:

> To love at all is to be vulnerable. Love anything, and your heart will
> certainly be wrung and possibly be broken. If you want to make sure
> of keeping it intact, you must give your heart to no-one...Wrap it
> carefully around...lock it up safe in the casket or coffin of your selfish-
> ness. But in that casket...it will change. It will not be broken; it will
> become unbreakable...the alternative to tragedy, or at least the risk of
> tragedy, is damnation. The only place outside heaven where you can
> be perfectly safe from all the perturbations of love is Hell.

(The Four Loves)

Two themes have emerged in the writing of this book: one is
concealment, the other is the word. Now I want to add a third:
what is central to the empowering moral curriculum is love. 'We
must love one another or die', said Auden, but of course, as he
later acknowledged, we must love another *and* die. It is a plati-
tude to say that the word *love* has to be rescued from the sentimental and vicious territory of the advertiser, the pornographer,
the soap-writer, the lyricist, to be recognised again for what it is:
the potential in all of us to make sacrifices to help another person
grow; or, less dramatically, in Weil's terms, 'just to hesitate for a
moment, in the face of another interest, to pay the attention that
the other deserves'.

We look in vain, of course, for references to the word 'love' in
official publications on PSME. Indeed, my palms sweat at the
thought of what would have been said on the PSE Guidelines
committee referred to in the Introduction if I had said, 'That's
enough of all this talk about accountability, audits, assessment.
PSME is really about love...Let's begin with the premise that we
must love the children and one another'.

'Love', John Ayto's *Dictionary of Word Origins* tells me, goes
back to an Indo-European word *'leobh'*, from which have
stemmed words that far outstrip 'love' in its more banal connota-
tions ('Isn't he a love?'). In fact, 'love' is associated with words
concerned with praise (the German *'lob'*, for example) and belief.
Thus, to love children is to treat them with the respect that is
realised in encouragement and faith. We praise and believe in
children by surrounding them with warm, rich environments,
and by doing the opposite of what MacNeice meant when he
talked about 'dragooning' individuals. To love them is to watch

what they do, be interested in it, to help them make it better. Love is the opposite of 'The low word "Don't"' (D. H. Lawrence, 'Snapdragon', *Selected Poems*). A. S. Neill brings together the etymological associations of the word love in his book *Summerhill:*

> The happiness and well-being of children depend on the degree of love and approval we give them...Being on the side of the child is giving love to the child – not possessive love – not sentimental love – just behaving to the child in such a way that the child feels you love him and approve of him...It is all a matter of faith in children...

Here is love in action. I asked a class of ten-year-old children to list the things (smells, sights, sounds, feelings, tastes) that remind each of them of someone s/he loves. 'What reminds you of her?' I asked. 'What makes you think of him? What books does she read, what newspapers does he buy? Close your eyes...'

Jennie's parents have just broken up, and she has left her father in Scotland and come to live in the south of England with her mother. The three themes of my book come together in her poem. She conceals nothing. In her words (redrafted and corrected with an editing friend) she expresses her love for her father. And, more significantly for us as teachers, she shows what love means in the classroom: the giving of opportunities like this one to grow in understanding of the World, and all its perturbations and perplexities.

Dad
I see you
in the midnight moon.
I feel you
in my mind telling me you're feeling good.
I taste you
in the night when we eat.
I hear you
at the crack of dawn
yawning.
I look at you
like I was just born yesterday.
I hug you
as if you're a teddy
all cuddly and soft.
You're invisible
but I can still see you at school.

She is in chains, of course. We all are. But she shows us here that, like Dylan Thomas's, her 'faith [is] as deathless as the outcry of the ruled sun'. This faith is in her father. Our faith in her is our love that does not sacrifice her to the past, does not see her only as an element in the future, but which lives with her today, and is a constant attention to her humanity, and to justice, and to truth.

References

Dannie Abse (1970), *Collected Poems*, London: Hutchinson.

W. H. Auden (1976), *Collected Poems*, London: Faber.

John Ayto (1990), *Dictionary of Word Origins*, London: Bloomsbury.

Stephen Ball (1990), *Foucault and Education*, London: Routledge.

Tony Booth, Will Swann, Mary Masterson and Patricia Potts (1992), *Curricula for Diversity in Education*, London: Routledge/Open University.

Encyclopaedia Britannica (1963), *An anthology of pieces from the early editions of Encyclopaedia Britannica*, London: Encyclopaedia Brittanica.

Alan Brownjohn (1983), *Collected Poems*, London: Hutchinson.

Sandy Brownjohn (1983), *What rhymes with secret?*, London: Hodder and Stoughton.

Sandy Brownjohn (1989), *The ability to name cats*, London: Hodder and Stoughton.

Charles Causley (1975), *Collected Poems*, London: Macmillan.

Alec Clegg and Barbara Megson (1968), *Children in Distress*, London, Penguin.

Cedric Cullingford (1994), 'The Attitudes of Children to their Environment', *Cambridge Journal of Education*, Volume 24, No. 1

John Danby (1940), Approach to Poetry, London: Heinemann.

Bronwyn Davies (1989), *Frogs and Snails and Feminist Tales*, London: Allen and Unwin.

Denise Dennis and Susan Willmarth (1984), *Black History for Beginners*, London: Writers and Readers.

Mary Jane Drummond (1993), *Assessing Children's Learning*, London: David Fulton Publishers.

T. S. Eliot (1939), *The Idea of a Christian Society*, London: Faber.

Michele Elliott (1991), *Feeling Happy Feeling Safe: A Safety Guide for Young Children*, London: Hodder & Stoughton.

Erich Fromm (1942), *The Fear of Freedom*, London: Routledge and Kegan Paul.

Bernard T. Harrison (1983), *Learning through Writing*, London: NFER-Nelson.

Angela Huth (editor) (1985), *Island of the Children*, London: Orchard Books.

Susan Isaacs (1930), *Intellectual Growth in Young Children*, London: Routledge and Kegan Paul.

Ronald Jeffcoate (1984), *Ethnic Minorities and Education*, London: Harper and Row.

James Joyce (1975), *A Portrait of the Artist as a Young Man*, London: Penguin.

Roland King (1979), *All Things Bright and Beautiful*, Chichester: John Wiley.

Simon Knott (editor) (1993), *Sight of the Road Home*, Ipswich: deshil holles eamus.

Peter Lang (editor) (1988), *Thinking about Personal and Social Education in the Primary School* , Oxford: Blackwell.

Philip Larkin (1986), *Collected Poems*, London: Faber.

D. H. Lawrence (1958), *Love Poems*, London: Studio Vista.

Dennis Lee (1993), *Jelly Belly*, Glasgow: Blackie.

C. S. Lewis (1960), *The Four Loves*, London: Bles.

David McNamara (1994), *Classroom Pedagogy and Primary Practice*, London: Routledge.

Louis MacNeice (1966), *Collected Poems*, London: Faber.

Hilary Minns (1985), *Alice in Genderland*, Sheffield: National Association for the Teaching of English.

Toni Morrison (1993), *Playing in the Dark*, London: Picador.

National Association for Pastoral Care in Education (1989), *Personal-Social Education and the National Curriculum*, NAPCE.

A S Neill (1968), *Summerhill*, London: Penguin.

Open University (1970), *The Yorubas of Nigeria*, Milton Keynes: The Open University.

Iona and Peter Opie (1959), *The Lore and Language of Schoolchildren*, Oxford: Oxford University Press.

Iona and Peter Opie (1985), *The Singing Game*, Oxford: Oxford University Press.

Andrew Pollard (1987), *Children and their Primary Schools*, Lewes: Falmer Press.

154

Malcolm Ross (1993), 'Children's Vision', *The Times Educational Supplement*, 19 March.

Meg Rutherford and Polly Richardson (1992), *Animal Poems*, Hemel Hempstead: Simon and Schuster.

Dawn and Fred Sedgwick (1993), *Drawing to Learn*, London: Hodder and Stoughton.

Fred Sedgwick (1986), 'Chipping at the Monolith', *Curriculum* .

Fred Sedgwick (1989), *Here Comes the Assembly Man*, Lewes: Falmer Press.

Fred Sedgwick (1992), 'Stories to dine out on', *The Times Educational Supplement*, September.

Fred Sedgwick (1991), *Lies*, Liverpool: Headland

Fred Sedgwick (1993), *The Expressive Arts*, London: David Fulton Publishers.

Frank Shaw (1970), *You Know me Auntie Nelly*, London: Wolfe.

Frank Smith (1982), *Writing and the Writer*, London: Heinemann.

Peter K. Smith and David Thompson (1991), *Practical Approaches to Bullying*, London: David Fulton Publishers.

Paula Sorhaindo (1993), *Pulse Rock*, Stevenage: Bowes Lyon House.

Wole Soyinka (1967), *Idanre and other poems*, London: Methuen.

Suffolk County Council (undated), *Guidelines for Personal and Social Education*.

Delwyn and Eva Tattum (1992), *Social Education and Personal Development*, London: David Fulton Publishers.

Frank Tuohy (1976), *Yeats*, London: Macmillan.

Martin Waddell (1990), *Grandma's Bill*, Hemel Hempstead: Simon and Schuster.

Alice Walker (1988), *To Hell with Dying*, London: Hodder and Stoughton.

Keith Waterhouse (1957), *There is a Happy Land*, London: Michael Joseph.

Stephen Waterhouse (1991), *First Episodes: Pupil careers in the early years of school*, Lewes: Falmer Press.

Liz Waterland (1994), *Not a Perfect Offering: a new school year*, Stroud: Thimble Press.

John White (1990), *Education and the Good Life: Beyond the National Curriculum*, London: Kogan Page.

Marian Whitehead (1993), 'Born Again Phonics and the Nursery Rhyme Revival,' *English in Education*, Autumn 1993

Index

DATE DUE			
JUL 15 '96			
AUG 05 '96			
AUG 2 5 1997			